INFINITE WAY LETTERS

Except the Lord build the house, they labour in vain that build it.

Psalm 127

Illumination dissolves all material ties and binds men together with the golden chains of spiritual understanding: it acknowledges only the leadership of the Christ; it has no ritual or rule but the divine, impersonal, universal Love; no other worship than the inner flame that is ever lit at the shrine of Spirit. This union is the free state of spiritual brotherhood. The only restraint is the discipline of Soul; therefore, we know liberty without license; we are a united universe without physical limits; a divine service to God without ceremony or creed. The illumined walk without fear—by Grace.

From the book, *The Infinite Way*, published by George Allen & Unwin Ltd.

The
INFINITE WAY LETTERS
1959

By
Joel S. Goldsmith

DeVorss & Company, Publishers

ISBN: 0-87516-631-8

Originally published in 1960
Second DeVorss & Company printing, 1993

DeVorss & Company, Publisher
P.O. Box 550
Marina del Rey, CA 90294

Printed in the United States of America

CONTENTS

5

INDIVIDUAL RESPONSIBILITY

WHEN children are no longer children, the responsibilities of adulthood fall upon their shoulders, and sometimes they come upon sad days because, even though they have reached the number of years which should be the measure of maturity, they are not always prepared for that responsibility. This is doubly true of truth-students. Very few of them are ready for the responsibilities of adulthood in truth, despite the fact that they may have been studying truth for ten, twenty, thirty, or forty years, because the number of years of study is no barometer of the spiritual maturity of a student.

You face a great responsibility when you come to a place in consciousness where your every word becomes a law unto yourself. No longer can you consider yourself a truth-student and at the same time violate truth in your thinking or in your living. Such failure to live truth may not carry with it too severe a penalty as long as this truth is merely a mental process or as long as it is something you think and then mouth as meaningless platitudes.

From the minute, however, that you grow up in truth and realize, "This is really true. I am the child of God; I am the offspring of God; God does constitute my being, and there is a Presence that goes before me to make the crooked places straight. I know now from watching my own life that there is an Influence in my life overshadowing me, that there is a Power over, above, and beyond anything human, physical, or mental"; from that moment you are really an adult in truth, and from then on you are obligated to live the words that you utter, or you will find truth to be a double-edged sword.

Just as human freedom and individual liberty entail serious responsibilities, so does spiritual freedom. Far too many people still think of freedom or liberty as license, the freedom to do anything they want to do, not realizing that freedom really means the freedom to live so that all may enjoy liberty—the same liberty and freedom you enjoy, the same liberty and freedom you want for yourself —so that all may be free to unite for the good of all. Therefore, inherent in liberty and freedom is the responsibility to uphold one another and the responsibility to stand in freedom with one another.

This is even more true of spiritual freedom, but such spiritual freedom can be achieved and retained only as spiritual maturity is achieved. This spiritual freedom, however, does not mean that a person is free to ignore the laws of God and do anything he may want to do. On the contrary, it places a deep responsibility upon him to love his neighbor as himself. It is the responsibility of every truth-student to attain spiritual maturity and show forth spiritual freedom to the world, because no one can help another, no one can love another, except in proportion as he, himself, has arrived at a place of spiritual realization; no one can give spiritual help to another unless he, himself, is spiritually endowed.

Spiritual Endowment Is a Prerequisite
to World Service

The first rule of spiritual wisdom is to forget the world: Forget about doing good in the world; forget your fellow-man. Concern yourself, first of all, with establishing your own spiritual integrity and with realizing your own spiritual identity. Be spiritually endowed, and then, automatically, you become your brother's keeper and you will be putting into practice loving your neighbor as yourself, because spiritual endowment is like the atmosphere of God: It is a rich perfume which escapes from you without any conscious effort. Then you do not have to go up and down the world being a "do-gooder." The mere fact that you are in the world means that some degree of spiritual power is flowing out from you, elevating human consciousness, even at the very time when you cannot see a visible result.

You have no idea what a widespread influence the word you speak this very day may have, but its influence will only be in the measure of your own spiritual endowment. If, instead of concerning yourself with "saving the world," you concern yourself primarily with your own spiritual unfoldment, then, in some miraculous way, God will provide ways and means for the truth you have realized to pour out of your mouth into somebody else's ear—but only because of your own spiritual attainments. You should have but one purpose and that is the development of your own spiritual capacity and spiritual endowment, bringing into activity in your consciousness the spiritual Presence and Power. What use God makes of that spiritual capacity after you develop it is God's business. As in the case of the first years in the training of a concert artist, whose function is not to go out looking for concert engagements, but to practice scales; so your function is to develop your own spiritual capacity.

Establish a Conscious Awareness of the Presence Daily

It becomes your function to maintain a conscious oneness with the Christ of your inner being, knowing that the Christ is the Son of God and is forever one with the Father. When you awaken in the morning, you will say to yourself, "Please, Father, do not let me make the mistake of leaving this room until I have consciously realized Thy presence." Later, before leaving your home, comes the reminder, "Father, do not let me leave here under my own steam; let me have the assurance of Your presence," and you sit down again for that moment of contact.

Acquire the habit of turning your thought to the realization that your dependence is on the Invisible, not the visible, that you do not live by bread alone or by anything in the external realm, but that you live by Grace, by every word that proceedeth out of the mouth of God. From the moment you make that a consistent practice, you are an expanding consciousness.

If you have made your conscious contact with God, you will find that every single day God will speak to you: "*I* am with you; fear not. Go about your business; *I* will be there ahead of you." There will always be something that will be in the nature of an assurance that you are not walking through this life alone or living on your own strength, that you are not working merely with your own limited intelligence. Always there will be a guiding Influence that will know just one thing more than you, yourself, know, that will empower you with one more degree of strength than you, yourself, possess.

As you make your contact with that Presence, first in lesser degree and later in greater degree, It begins to live your life, and you find yourself acknowledging, "I am alive and living, but there is Something more than the little 'I' functioning in me; there is Something more than that personal 'I,' directing, guiding, prospering, and strengthening me."

A dozen times a day remember that, as a mere human being, you are cut off from your Source. Therefore, make your conscious union, your conscious contact, and persist in it even though there may be intermittent periods of discord and inharmony. It was Paul who said in substance, "I cannot declare yet that I have arrived at the fullness, but at least forgetting those things which are past, I am going to go forward."

Through the activity of truth in your consciousness, you will maintain your life under Grace, but do not think for a single moment that on this plane you will ever advance so high spiritually that temptation in one form or another cannot come to you. That temptation, however, is more likely to come in the guise of good than of evil. I doubt that there are many people who have been really touched by the

Spirit who are very seriously tempted by what the world calls evil, but I have seen many of them tempted by the world's good—by fame, wealth, or ease.

Live the Principles of The Infinite Way

There comes a time in the life of every student of truth when he must live the words he declares, because truth must be lived and not merely used as a shield or a cloak, or as a garment to be put on or off at will. Whatever measure of truth the coming generations may accept will be due to what you and I do today. If you and I cannot successfully demonstrate spiritual living and spiritual healing, we have nothing to give to the world. If you believe that this teaching has the possibility of bringing spiritual harmony into your experience, manifested as harmony of health, supply, companionship, and all relationships, you must certainly feel that it has that possibility for the world.

If you believe The Infinite Way is a message which can be made practicable in daily experience, a responsibility rests on your shoulders to live it and to demonstrate it. It is not a responsibility that you owe me or The Infinite Way. The responsibility is first to yourself and then to all those who are seeking a way out of their human difficulties.

The kingdom of God is within *you*, and if you will make the necessary sacrifice and give the requisite devotion, you will be able to make contact with this kingdom of God within you and draw forth harmony, wholeness, and completeness. Recognize then that you do have a responsibility, and that responsibility is to demonstrate the principles of The Infinite Way and, thereby, show forth the personal integrity which is an inseparable part of the Message.

Man shall not live by bread alone, but by every word that proceedeth out of the mouth of God.[1] . . . Take no thought for your life, what ye shall eat, or what ye shall drink; nor yet for your body, what ye shall put on.[2] . . . Your Father knoweth that ye have need of these things. . . . It is your Father's good pleasure to give you the kingdom.[3]

These statements indicate that you need take no thought, you need have no concern for the necessities of life—for supply, health, home, companionship, or transportation—because these things are effects: They are the bread, the form. There is an invisible Something, and it is Its responsibility to provide, govern, maintain, and sustain the harmony of your being. Therefore, your only responsibility is to demonstrate this Infinite Invisible which we call God. Demonstrate the Spirit of God which raised up Jesus Christ from the dead, and It will quicken your mortal bodies also. Demonstrate that, and you will have demonstrated the principle of The Infinite Way.

"For by grace are ye saved"[4]—by this Spirit within you, and when the Spirit of God dwells in you, then do you become the Son of God. Then are you spiritual, eternal, immortal, and undying. That part of you which is of the flesh dies daily, and you are reborn of the Spirit. You learn then that this

[1] Matthew 4:4.   [2] Matthew 6:25.
[3] Luke 12:30, 32.   [4] Ephesians 2:8.

new you, the "rebirthed" you, was never born. It merely came to light when the Spirit of God touched you. It is after the Spirit of God has touched you that you become the child of God, and then you sow to the Spirit and reap life everlasting.

The Spirit of God first touched you when you were turned to a spiritual teaching. Of your own self, you would not turn to God, but when the Spirit of God touches you, It begins to destroy that personal sense of self, and you begin to "die daily" to that which, heretofore, you had been. All the things which have constituted the major part of your life—the pleasures that you thought you could not live without, your position in life, your wealth, or your intellectual attainments—now begin to be less and less important. One day you awaken and find that their place has been supplanted by an inner drive, an inner desire to know God, an inner devotion to the things of God, and an inner companionship with those on the spiritual path.

Today can be that day of transition for us. If we remember this day as the time when we made the decision to forget "those things which are behind, and [to reach] for those things which are before, [to] press toward the mark for the prize of the high calling of God in Christ Jesus," a year from now we shall have to admit that a transformation of our life is in progress. The human sense of life will never again touch us so deeply: we shall never again be able to hate or to love quite so intensely as before; we shall neither grieve nor rejoice with the same intensity of human emotion. The depth of our vision will continue to bring forth greater and greater spiritual light, wisdom, and guidance, so that every day will be a day of deeper discernment, a day of greater living in the atmosphere of God than the preceding day. This work will serve as a foundation on which we may build the temple of our body and home, the temple of our individual experience—a temple not made with hands, eternal in the heavens.[1]

The "old man" who has not had the time for spiritual living is beginning to die; the "old man" who has been devoting his life to the baubles of life is dying. This is what happens as one finds his way to this path. It is natural that along the way he may receive some baubles and enjoy them, but he is not seeking them, he is not devoting his life to trying to achieve them. The heart, soul, mind, and Spirit within are devoted to but one thing: to find Him whom to know aright is life eternal, and to rest in Him.

Regardless of what sacrifices must be made, regardless of what engagements must be foregone, regardless of what travels must be undertaken, those on the spiritual path will never rest until they rest in Him, because the Spirit of God has touched them. The world finds rest and relaxation in movies, television, radio, sports, music, and mystery stories, but, even though those on the spiritual path may enjoy such diversions occasionally, they cannot find rest or peace in them. The Spirit has already touched them, and their rest is found in this search.

In The Infinite Way, you show forth by the life you lead that there is Something which makes it

[1] From the author's *The Art of Meditation* (New York: Harper and Brothers, 1956), pp. 135-136; (London: George Allen and Unwin, Ltd., 1956), pp. 135-136.

possible for you to say that man shall not live by bread alone. There is Something beyond bread— beyond form.

I need take no thought for my life, because there is a Something concerning Itself about me, a Something whose pleasure it is to give me the kingdom. There is a Something, an I which lives, and yet not "I"! It is the Christ, the Spirit of God in me which lives my life. It is that Something beyond form, but which appears as form, filling the seas with fish, the earth with gems, the air with birds, the skies with stars.

Exercise Your God-Given Dominion

Once you have been touched by this Presence and Power, you must live by It. It must become your experience—the very substance of your body. You do not live by the organs and functions of the body. The organs and functions of the body live by It—the activity of God. If there were not an It, your heart could not beat and your blood could not flow, because it is this It, this indefinable Something, which keeps the organs and functions of the body operating. Through your acceptance of a universal belief that the organs and functions of the body govern your life, you have lost your hope of immortality here and now. The dominion given you by God in the beginning over everything on earth, including your body, you have surrendered to the body by admitting, "Oh, no, I haven't dominion over you; you have dominion over me."

It is similar to a thief going before a judge in court, attempting to justify himself by saying, "I didn't steal; it was my hand that did it." Obviously any such attempt would be ridiculous. Everyone knows that a hand cannot steal, and yet you are guilty of much the same mistake when you say, "He is dead because his heart has stopped beating." Some day you will recognize that your heart only stops beating when you give your consent: It is the *I* which has dominion, and that *I* is not a man or a woman; that *I* is the principle of life which formed the body in the beginning and which is your identity.

The body did not form itself. *I*, the Spirit of God in man, formed it. "Know ye not that your body is the temple of the Holy Ghost?"[1] Or have you forgotten that this body is not yours, but God's? God has dominion over it. The *I* of your being, that which is your true being, has dominion, but you have retreated into a position where you have permitted your body to have dominion over you.

Some day you must awaken spiritually. For example, you would not let your body steal. In that respect, you are in full control of it; but, because you have fallen afoul of the universal belief handed down through the ages that the body is something which governs and controls your life, you give up the government of your body and let it say, "I am sick," or, "I am old." Life governs your body: The body does not govern life. The same principle that raised up Jesus Christ from the dead will quicken also your mortal body.

Practitioners in The Infinite Way only succeed as they arrive at a state of consciousness in which they perceive the reason for their faith. No one

[1] I Corinthians 6:19.

arrives at the practitioner-state of consciousness who has not seen through the physical sense of existence to the absolute truth. When he has achieved that vision, he has what the world calls "the courage of his convictions" which actually is not that at all, but a knowledge of the principles underlying life.

A doctor, watching a practitioner of spiritual healing at the bedside of a dying patient, may say, "You have a great deal of courage not to resort to some material remedy," but I can say to you that no courage at all is involved. What is involved is attaining a state of awareness in which there is an absolute conviction that health is not dependent on the body, but that the body is dependent on an omnipresent state of health. Health is here and now; health is just as omnipresent as integrity, loyalty, or fidelity. The reason we are not experiencing health in its fullness is that instead of looking to health to govern the body, we have looked to the body to produce health.

"Choose you this day whom ye will serve."[1] Everyone who enters the spiritual path reaches a certain point in his experience, a certain day in which a choice must be made, a choice which brings with it the conviction, "I cannot go on this way forever; I cannot continue a partial reliance first in one direction and then in another." This is a difficult day for students because it is usually more comfortable to pursue a policy of vacillation from one extreme to another than to throw off the inertia so typical of humanhood and come to a place of decision.

[1] Joshua 24:15.

Every student on the spiritual path has proved that the body does not give health, nor does the body control health. It is health that controls the body, and health is a constituted part of your consciousness. All that the Father has is yours. Therefore, the immortality and eternality of the Father is the immortality and the eternality of individual being. That truth known and realized becomes the health of the body. It takes no courage to give up the use of material remedies the moment one realizes that his health is not dependent upon a form or an effect. It is not difficult to lose a fear of lack when it is realized that it is not money that constitutes the abundance of supply, but the realization of the ever presence of abundance which produces the forms of supply.

By virtue of having been born, you are under the law—the law of cause and effect, the law of environmental influences, the law of heredity, the law of infection and contagion, the law of sin, the law of disease, the law of wealth and poverty. By the mere fact of birth, you are subject to every human belief that exists anywhere on earth. But from the moment that you turned to truth, you have been freeing yourself from the law, bringing yourself under the grace of the Spirit. For a long, long time on this path, it will be necessary for you consciously to remember that you are removing yourself from under the law and bringing yourself under Grace.

Every day that you, by a conscious realization of God's grace, remove yourself from under the law and acknowledge yourself to be living under Grace, you are dying daily. As that process continues, there is less human reaction to life, and life is lived on an entirely different plane. The reactions are different, and the things of the world run off the shoulders without affecting you in any way.

Know the truth and the truth will make you free. From the moment you begin to understand that life functions this body and that supply is the source of the money you need and use, you are free of the fears of this world and, in a measure, you have overcome this world. The Master said, "I have overcome the world."[1] He did not overcome it by having the wealth of Midas, nor did he have a storehouse full of health upon which he could draw. He overcame this world by knowing that right where he stood was holy ground and that right there was that Spirit in man which maintained him. It is that Spirit, the Spirit which is your consciousness, that produces harmonious forms.

There is only one activity and that is the activity of consciousness. There is only one real sense, consciousness, of which the five physical senses—sight, hearing, taste, touch, and smell—are but extensions. Each one of these senses functions in a different way. Each part of the body functions in a different way: the hands in one way, the feet another, the right hand one way, and the left hand another, each complementing the other and forming a complete whole. Every part of you is an extension of consciousness. That consciousness is God, and, therefore, God is functioning through your mind and body, and through every activity of your life.

In every phase of your experience, you can open

[1] John 16:33.

yourself to the infinite Source of being, and your life will be lived infinitely, spiritually, harmoniously, and perfectly. "The kingdom of God is within you.[1] . . . I and my Father are one.[2] . . . Call no man your father upon the earth: for one is your Father, which is in heaven"[3]—God." The one Consciousness is your consciousness—God. The one Life is your life— God. Reach back and let It unfold, disclose, and reveal Itself; and It will live Its life as your life, and in that life infinity will be the measure of your demonstration.

*   *   *

ACROSS THE DESK

The Fourth Dimension of consciousness is attained only when, by the grace of God, we are enabled to relinquish the struggle for the attainment of things and conditions—effects—and abide only in the desire for the realization of God. Having God, we have all. Therefore, seek God alone and *let* the forms of good flow naturally into expression.

It is clear that many of our students are ready for this experience. When *Leave Your Nets* was published, I thought that that one printing would last forever because certainly only the most advanced students would want it or would be able to understand and appreciate it. Now only a few hundred copies remain, and after this present edition has been exhausted, *Leave Your Nets* will be out of print for a year or more because there are so many books in preparation which have precedence over this one. It is interesting to note that second printings have

[1] Luke 17:21.   [2] John 10:30.   [3] Matthew 23:9.

been made of *Consciousness Unfolding* and *The Master Speaks* in the new revised British editions.

The widespread interest in these publications is evidence that many are ready for progressive and forward steps in spiritual living. Just as the March and October, 1958, *Letters* and the chapter, "Love Thy Neighbor," in *Practicing the Presence*, epitomize the essential principles of Infinite Way spiritual healing, so *The Letters* of November and December, 1958, and of January and February, 1959, point the way for beginning the spiritual journey above words and thoughts. Let me emphasize, however, that without the foundation given in the March and October, 1958, *Letters* and "Love Thy Neighbor" in *Practicing the Presence*, this next step is almost impossible of attainment. There must be diligent application of these principles to every phase of human existence and some measure of success achieved in bringing to light spiritual harmony before a deeper understanding and realization of God can take place.

Why is this? Because a universal mesmerism—a material sense of life—grips the human mind causing it to behold and accept conditions of good and evil. This material sense is broken only as we perceive its nature as but "the arm of flesh"—nothingness or non-power. Until we attain such perception, we fight error, we struggle against evil, we pray to overcome sin, disease, and lack. By the recognition and practice of the principles of The Infinite Way, however, we learn to "resist not evil" and to abandon the chase for its opposite, and thereby find ourselves abiding in the atmosphere of divine Grace.

It really is possible to live by Grace. Blind faith will not attain it, nor will hoping or wishing. Even deserving it will not attain it. "Labour not for the meat which perisheth."[1] Leave the nets with which you seek to catch fish and "follow Me"—attain the realization that *I Am*. Fear not—the loaves and fishes will appear.

This New Year is a good time to turn within for contemplation and introspection: The elections held this last November remind us that "this world" still places its trust and confidence in "chariots and strong horses." The world still pins its faith and hope in might and in power; it still fears the might of "the armies of the alien." Have we given up hope in, and fear of, material force and mental power? Do we still believe that men and governments control the fate of mankind, or, after having voted to the highest of our convictions as good citizens, have we returned to abiding not in governments made by men, but rather in that Temple, that Consciousness, not made by hands?

A thousand million may fall at our left and more thousands of millions at our right—and fall they will—but it shall not come nigh those who no longer place their hope in "princes" or their faith in "man, whose breath is in his nostrils."[2] We cannot help our world by attempting to change things, conditions, or men, but only by a conscious contact with God through meditation, a contact which brings the very presence and activity of God into immediate experience.

Our students around the globe are now proving

[1] John 6:27.   [2] Isaiah 2:22.

that they can mitigate and even dissolve some evil conditions and bring harmony to light in their communities by the practice of meditation and through a conscious contact with God. Therefore, in every circumstance, bring the actual presence of God to the scene through meditation. By daily realization in meditation of God's grace here and now, be a light, not only to your family and fellow-students, but to your community—even to your enemy.

Except the Lord build the house, they labour in vain that build it.

—Psalm 127:1

Illumination dissolves all material ties and binds men together with the golden chains of spiritual understanding; it acknowledges only the leadership of the Christ; it has no ritual or rule but the divine, impersonal, universal Love; no other worship than the inner Flame that is ever lit at the shrine of Spirit. This union is the free state of spiritual brotherhood. The only restraint is the discipline of Soul; therefore, we know liberty without license; we are a united universe without physical limits; a divine service to God without ceremony or creed. The illumined walk without fear—by Grace.

—*The Infinite Way*.

We are united in a spiritual bond of consciousness, and the meditation of each of us is a benediction to all of us. And because we are "two or more" united in His consciousness, we shall lift *all* men unto us.

A LESSON TO SAM

Now, Sam, this lesson is important because it is not just a lesson for one day. If you are faithful in putting this lesson into practice, it will be sufficient for the rest of your life, even if you never receive another one from me.

I have been thinking about your going away to school and of how you will be able to live The Infinite Way when you are away from our personal influence, your mother's and mine, and when you may not do too much reading in my books. While I hope that you will do some reading each day, if only a page in one of my writings, even more would I like to have you learn this lesson, which I am about to give you, so well that, if you were alone on a desert island or out in a rubber boat in the middle of the ocean and had no person around you and no books with you, you could still survive and demonstrate your safety, your security, peace, food, clothing, housing, and everything necessary for your unfoldment.

I want to tell you the secret that has brought me happiness, joy, success, prosperity, and the ability to be of help to my fellow-men and to children throughout this world. I want you to know that secret so that you can go and do likewise.

Whenever you are faced with any problem,

whether it is one of health, one concerning your lessons at school, or let us say one that concerns your relationship with other boys in school or with your teachers, here is your first step: Get comfortable; close your eyes; put your feet on the floor; and now remember that God is closer to you than breathing, nearer than hands and feet. Right there, where you are standing or sitting or playing, God is. You have only to close your eyes, get quiet for a moment, and God will solve your problem.

It may sound strange to you that you don't have to tell God what your problem is or that you don't have to ask God for any favors, and that you don't even have to make any statements or affirmations: All you have to do is to close your eyes, get still for a moment, and realize that God is as close to you as inside your own chest. Then be patient for a few minutes, and the Spirit, Itself, will take over. If you need help with your lessons, that instruction will come forth very quickly, just as you have seen here in our work together that, when you have been stuck with a mathematical problem, instead of my working it out for you, we meditated. And then when you went back to the book, you found the answer as plainly stated there as if it had been written out especially for you.

So it is, if you have a problem in your studies or if there is some subject that you are not properly grasping, stop what you are doing for a moment, close your eyes, and realize that God is right here, closer to you than breathing. Wait for just a minute or two, and you will find that God, who is the divine intelligence of your being, knows that you are coming to Him, and what you are coming to Him for. Always remember that it is God's good pleasure to give you the answer. In fact, it is very much like a radio station: God is always talking to you; God is always revealing the answer to every problem, whether it concerns your lessons, your health, or your human relationships; but you cannot receive God's guidance, direction, protection, or support unless you are tuned in to accept it.

It is like your sitting here in this room and receiving instruction in spiritual wisdom from me. But suppose that you had your ears closed and weren't listening, or suppose you were outside playing, or suppose you were downtown at the movies, how then could you receive that which I so willingly offer you? The answer is: You couldn't.

Now, as a human father, I would gladly give you every spiritual secret I have, just as readily as I would give you every dollar I have, if these would prove a blessing to you. But do you not see that I cannot give you any of these things unless you are receptive to them, unless you are giving back in return your attention, your gratitude, your love, and your obedience?

Just so it is with God. You must give God obedience, attention, loving-ness, not by loving a God whom you cannot see, but by loving the boys and girls with whom you come in contact, and your teachers. Always remember, as you leave this home, that you are to express the same respect toward the boys and girls whom you meet as the mutual respect that you have witnessed taking place in this home. You know the love and the respect there is between your mother and me and between you and me; and you know that, when your mother and I go out into the world, we give this same love and this same respect to everyone we meet. That is the example you must follow and carry out into practice. And why? In order that you may receive God's grace, because even though God is present with you, you cannot receive God's grace unless love, joy, and respect fill your mind and your Soul.

Each one of us is responsible for himself. There is no God sitting up in a sky, looking down upon you and judging your actions; but there is a God-center within you that knows everything you do and which brings back to you that which you send out. Therefore, the love and the respect that you send out are the love and respect that you get back, and not only that, but they are pressed down and running over.

Now, even though you went out into the world and loved your neighbor as yourself and were humanly good in every way, this would not be enough, for that is only fulfilling the Ten Commandments, and what you are now being taught is how to fulfil the Sermon on the Mount.

The Infinite Way is really a revelation which says that you do not have to speak to God, but that you must have periods of the day or the night when you listen to God; and even though you may not hear a voice, remember that just by opening your ear to God and being silent for a minute or two you have permitted God to rush into that vacuum which you have created.

It operates like this: Close your eyes; put your feet on the floor; listen way down inside of yourself;

and then remember that this day which lies ahead of you is now God-governed, God-protected, God-maintained, and God-sustained because you have consciously opened your consciousness to the presence and the government of God. Remember that if you do not do this every morning you go out into the world just as a human being, subject to all the trials and tribulations of the human world, and without divine guidance.

Actually, at your age and with the teaching that you have had here in your home, you should be ready to have four periods a day—early in the morning, at noon, about dinner time, and before retiring—in which to take two minutes each time just to sit down and turn within and say, "Here I am, Father: Speak, Lord, Thy servant heareth. I am obedient to Thy will." And then just be still for one minute. I can promise you that if you do that, your life in school will be a success, and even more than that, you will be laying the foundation for a completely God-governed life.

What the world does not always understand is that it is not too important whether you go through church rituals or church forms of ceremony. A church can be helpful if you go to it with your mind open: It can be an opportunity for you to be quiet and hear the still small voice. Therefore, I say to you that if the boys in your school go to a church service, I would certainly suggest that you also go to the service—and remember, this is only a suggestion, for your life is free for you to make or to break—and if they go through a ritual, you go through it; if they go through forms of worship, you go through them. Because all of you are united in that service in the name of God, it can do you a great deal of good; but the real good comes because you are there to acknowledge God's grace and God's glory.

The important thing that I want you to see, Sam, is that, in any instance and in every instance, at any moment of the day or night, God is instantly available to you merely by closing your eyes and inwardly listening. I'm trying to emphasize that it isn't the statements you make, it isn't talking to God, it isn't asking God. None of that is necessary because the secret that I have learned is that God is infinite intelligence and He already knows our needs, even before we do. The way God fulfils our needs is through our inner listening—not through our talking, not through our saying words or thinking thoughts, because the Master said, "Take no thought for your life, what ye shall eat; neither for the body, what ye shall put on.... Your Father knoweth that ye have need of these things. . . . For it is your Father's good pleasure to give you the kingdom." Do you see that?

It is His good pleasure to give you the kingdom, and God does not even hold you in punishment for your sins. Even though you make a mistake, even though you commit a sin, if you are truly repentant in the sense that you realize that you have sinned and that it wasn't right, in that instant you are forgiven. You do not carry around the penalty any longer than you carry around the obstinacy of believing you are right when you know in your heart and Soul you are wrong. Do you understand that? You cannot go around and do wrong and not acknowledge it to yourself and expect that you can receive God's grace.

You receive God's grace every time you acknowledge within yourself, "I know I've done wrong," or perhaps, "I don't know that I've done wrong, but if I have, God, wipe it out, because it wasn't intentional. I never mean to do wrong, but always want to do unto others as I would have others do unto me." In that way, you purify yourself. I have been healed of illnesses merely by asking God's forgiveness for my sins; and of course, my sins are not major ones because you know that is not our mode of living. But whatever it is—when we are guilty of holding people in criticism or condemnation, or when we are not loving enough or forgiving enough —we are sinning against the Holy Spirit. So it is a wholesome thing once in a while to go to God and say, "I realize that humanly I haven't been perfect; therefore, forgive my sins, forgive my trespasses, and let's start all over again."

In this way, Sam, you will learn the greatest lesson that I have ever learned, and that is that the place whereon I stand is holy ground. God is right here where I am, and God is available the very minute that I stop talking and stop thinking and turn within in humility, acknowledging God's grace, God's power, God's Spirit within me, and then relax for just a minute or two and let that Spirit take over. That really is all there is to the whole Infinite Way.

All the writings of The Infinite Way are only for the purpose of leading people to this revelation of God's omnipresence and ever availability, without taking thought, without words, without anything except the humility to sit or stand or lie down, close the eyes, and acknowledge, "I, of my own self, can do nothing. 'The Father . . . me, he doeth the works. . . . Speak, Lord; for thy servant heareth,' " and then wait just one minute or two minutes before you get up and go about your task. If you learn to practice this four times a day as I suggest, it will not be long before you realize that you are doing it many more than four times a day.

And now, just one thing more. Never forget that one of the greatest statements in the Bible is, "In all thy ways acknowledge him, and he shall direct thy paths." This means that, when you awaken in the morning, your first thought has to be, "Thank You, Father, for this glorious day that is before me." When you eat, you stop for that blink of the eyes as you know we do here in the home, and even if all you say to yourself is, "Happy days," "Good appetite," or whatever it is that you want to say with your lips, you mean with your Soul, "Thank You, God, for setting this table." Right?

So it is that when you go out to play blink your eyes, and realize, "Thank You, Father, for Your presence." When you go swimming, when you participate in sports, when you do your homework, acknowledge God's presence there; and then you won't have to rely on your own ability because, if you do, I can tell you in advance that you will not be equal to it. I know because, alone, I am not equal to my job. If it were not for God's grace at every step that I take, this work that you witness here could not be done.

Well, Sam, I don't know that anyone could add anything to this, but if so, I'm sure that it will be done some day. I am going to have this typed for you so that you can read it over once in awhile as a reminder. This is the secret of life and, with this that I am giving you now, you can carve out for yourself a grand life of service to others, be a blessing to yourself and a joy to your parents, and the whole thing for the glory of God.

Always remember, God made you, and therefore any good thing you do is to the glory of God. Your parents brought you into this expression and are your human guardians, supporting, supplying, and protecting you; and on the human plane, every good thing you do becomes a glory to your parents, something in which they can take pride. And so, you have your spiritual Father, in whom you should glory and to whom you should give glory, and you have your human parents, to whom you should give the opportunity to glory in your accomplishments.

BE A TRANSPARENCY FOR GOD

God is absent from the human scene except where the consciousness of an individual becomes illumined, and then the Light which is God shines through that transparency. From the moment Moses had his great illumination, his facial expression and bodily appearance changed; in fact, his whole life changed to such an extent that it was possible for him to liberate the Hebrews from Pharaoh and lead them across the desert and through the wilderness into some measure of freedom. Until the illumination of Moses, God was absent from the experience of the

Hebrews, and it was only through the enlightened consciousness of one man, Moses, that He became visible and tangible to them.

When you as an individual become illumined, you are then the transparency through which God reaches, not only your experience, but the experience of those with whom you come in contact. One individual such as a Moses or a Jesus receives the light and plays a tremendous part in history, bringing light, illumination, and human betterment to the world; but because there are not more men and women of the world who are touched by that same Light, the world retrogrades and goes back again to its slavish devotion to material forms.

As human beings, we are barriers to God, and God cannot break through, because God cannot manifest Himself on earth through a human being engrossed in materiality: It is only the human being who has "died" sufficiently to his humanhood who is capable of receiving light or spiritual illumination, thereby becoming the transparency through which God can appear. And then it is that the grace of God penetrates the particular part of the world where that spiritual light is. Those people who have received some measure of spiritual light—and there are some in every part of the world—are a blessing and a benediction to their particular world.

Paul felt that he had not yet achieved, but forgetting those limitations which were behind, he said, "I press toward the mark for the prize of the high calling of God in Christ Jesus."[1] No one can yet claim to be Omniscience, yet everyone can claim

[1] Philippians 3:14.

Omniscience to be the measure of his mind, Soul, Spirit, and body. Everyone can reach back into that Omniscience which is his individual being, and let It flow, and It will come forth in the measure of his understanding today. Tomorrow, It will come forth in greater measure and next year in still greater measure. There can never be a limit to the unfolding consciousness which you are when you go beyond the reasoning, thinking mind.

Only in your meditations are you receptive to the flow of divine Wisdom, and only through these meditations can you develop the sense of being used by God, of being an instrument through which God flows. Only in meditation can you let go and rest in the realization:

Thank You, Father, that there is nothing to heal, nothing to overcome, and nobody to reform: There is only a resting in Thee, a resting in the sufficiency of Thy grace. In that resting, I am no longer under the law of good and evil, no longer under the law of strength and weakness, no longer under the law of threescore years and ten, no longer under the law of the calendar or men's beliefs which change year by year: I am subject only to Thy grace.

What doth the Lord thy God require of thee, but to fear the Lord thy God, to walk in all his ways, and to love him, and to serve the Lord thy God with all thy heart and with all thy soul.

Deuteronomy 10:12

What doth the Lord require of thee, but to do justly, and to love mercy, and to walk humbly with thy God?

Micah 6:8

Execute true judgment, and shew mercy and compassions every man to his brother:

37

And oppress not the widow, nor the fatherless, the stranger, nor the poor; and let none of you imagine evil against his brother in your heart.

Speak ye every man the truth to his neighbour; execute the judgment of truth and peace in your gates:

And let none of you imagine evil in your hearts against his neighbour.

Zechariah 7:9, 10; 8:16, 17

Let the power of Truth use you. Let the power and the presence of God use you. Be a transparency; be an instrument through which the divine Power flows.

ACROSS THE DESK

Have you realized the secret of the December, 1958, *Letter*? Do not file that *Letter* away until it has yielded at least some measure of what it contains.

My mail always abounds in questions, and the most frequent question is, "Why? Why do I not make more rapid progress? Why do I not receive healing? Why do I not find companionship or home or supply?" The answer may not always be the same, but nearly always the question, "Why?" can be answered as follows: Consciously or unconsciously, the questioner is seeking something. This may be the natural thing for the beginner since most of us come to the search for God because of some problem or some lack in our lives. And usually our problem has been solved or our lack met through the consciousness of a dedicated practitioner or teacher.

Did the solution of our problem turn us to the search for the principle of the demonstration, or did it merely send us out seeking more demonstrations?

To what extent have our many healings inspired us with either a deep love of God or a craving to know God aright?

There is but one solution to our unsolved problems: the attainment of spiritual realization, the awakening of the Christ-nature within us. Each one of us must eventually embark on the search for the Holy Grail—the awakened consciousness.

There is but one way to world peace, and that is to live by Grace instead of by the sword. But the world cannot live by Grace until individually and collectively it has received inner illumination.

Inner light, or Soul-awakening, is attained as we turn from the chase after health, home, and companionship and seek diligently the awareness or revelation of our spiritual nature. Our study, the practice of The Infinite Way principles, and meditation will achieve this for us, and never again will we find it necessary to seek the things of "this world."

Go back, again and again, to the December, 1958, *Letter*. Let its spirit fill you. It contains my dream for your attainment. For many years I have had this vision, and nowhere in my writings is it so clearly set forth. When you read this *Letter* of December, you are glimpsing my vision.

Some of our students who have been with me many years will now understand what I meant when I told them that I know nothing about how to get health or supply. One thing only do I know, and that is that the longing to know God eventually became an inner spiritual experience, and ever since then it has been possible for me to commune within and to receive impartations of Truth, Light, and

Grace. Outwardly this has appeared, not only as my health, supply, and companionship, but also as the entire Infinite Way activity.

Another answer to this question of "Why do I not make greater or faster progress?" is that the word God too often is a stumbling block. The old theological sense of God persists: We consciously or unconsciously continue to think of God as some super-figure who can and does withhold our good, either for some sin of omission or commission, or because we have not discovered the correct form of prayer, or, even as some people believe, the correct posture or breathing, or we think we are not sufficiently "good."

Let us begin here with the understanding that we are not seeking God for any reason. Actually, we are not really seeking God, since I and the Father are already one, and our need is only for a *realization* of this oneness.

In the stillness of our being, there is a transcendental Power, a spiritual Activity, which dissolves the mistakes of mind and body and changes our nature and bodily form and functions. This transcendental Presence is awakened in us as our spiritual reading, hearing, study, and meditations become a larger part of our daily experience. This transcendental Activity takes over our experience in proportion as we relax from mental thought-taking, as we rest from trying to make something happen by virtue of our thoughts or statements, and as we succeed in being inwardly still.

Since this power and presence of the Spirit is never outside of you or beyond your reach, since it does not have to be struggled for, you will attain it more quickly by knowing that it is already closer than breathing, and then by relaxing and resting in It. You do not need words or thoughts to bring It to your experience. It is already there. Know this, and in the assurance of It, rest and relax.

Look up the word "transcendental" in your dictionary and live with this word, always associating it with your own inner being. You carry this Presence with you wherever you go, and It will govern every phase of your life—as you live It, love It, relax and rest in It. This transcendental Power is what the world of religion calls "God with us," or the Christ. But It is more than this: It is *your* spiritual nature, the gift of God in you.

A Program of Study for 1959

During November, obedient to the "still small voice" heard in Holland, I remained at home in retreat at Halekou. Then in December, a number of students came to Hawaii from the Mainland for periods of meditation and instruction; but throughout this entire period, the unfoldment begun in Holland has continued, and where and when it will end, I do not know at present, but I shall continue to remain here at home until the Voice tells me to travel.

Meanwhile, in order to prepare for whatever further work is given us to do, I ask all of our students who have access to tape recording groups to study well the 1956 work which embodies the revelation on the first and second chapters of Genesis and the Sermon on the Mount. Following that, a thorough study should be made of the 1957 Halekou Classes and the 1958 work which includes the Adelaide Healing Class, the two 1958 Chicago Classes, the 1958 New York Class, the Manchester, England, Closed Class, the London Advanced Class, and the London Open Class. With this study, you will be ready for anything that may be given you to do, and certainly you will be active in the healing work.

For those who do not have access to the tape classes, there must be further preparation through the study and practice of *The Art of Meditation* and *Practicing the Presence* and the study of the healing work found in *The 1957 Infinite Way Letters* and the March, October, and December, 1958, *Letters*, as well as the chapters, "Love Thy Neighbor," in *Practicing the Presence* and, "The New Horizon," in *The Infinite Way*.

I realize that this is a difficult schedule—one which demands dedication to the work—and, therefore, I shall expect only those students to follow it who are intent upon God-realization. To such serious students, no effort will be too great to attain that goal through the development of spiritual consciousness.

Is it clear to all Infinite Way students that spiritual healing and harmony in daily living are the fruitage of an attained spiritual consciousness, and that this consciousness is developed and achieved only by the study of the correct letter of truth, by the practice of these healing principles, and by contemplation and meditation leading to conscious communion with the Source of your being—the Kingdom within you?

THE SECRET OF THE RESURRECTION

THE majority of people in this world believe that, because they wake up in the morning, manage to stay alive during the day, and finally are able to go to sleep at night, they are living. That is not living: That is merely existing, but the hopelessness of such existence is not apparent to the average person until he discovers what a real living of life is.

Oriental philosophy refers to the endless routine of waking up in the morning, struggling through the day, and then being so grateful to get into bed at night, only in order to repeat the process the next day, as being on the wheel of life. It is like a merry-go-round—round and round it goes, but it never goes anywhere. Round and round, yet standing still! That is typical of the human being who lives a life of waking up in the morning, struggling through the day, and happily going back to bed at night. And why is he so happy to get into bed at night? Because he is going to wake up in the morning and go no place all over again. It is fruitless—an endless struggle for survival without any real purpose.

There is a wholly different life that comes to the awakened soul, a life in which living is not just a succession of waking up and going to sleep, eating and drinking, but in which there is a succession of delights during both day and night. It is the life in which the "my peace I give unto you"[1] is not an idle dream, nor is it an impossible one.

Some people imagine that "My peace" is merely a round of days and nights without pain or without lack, but it is more than that, much more. There may even be some problems after the state of consciousness known as "My peace" has been reached, but they are not too important when one has the vision of the new world—of "My kingdom," that Kingdom which is not of this world. As a matter of fact, even if a person's days were filled wholly with happy human experiences, that is not the spiritual kingdom. The spiritual kingdom is neither lo here, nor lo there, nor is it health or material affluence. The spiritual kingdom is something that no human being can ever encompass because a human being has only the mind as a means of cognition, and the mind of man cannot encompass the realm of God: Spiritual consciousness is necessary for that, and through spiritual consciousness comes the resurrection from humanhood into "My kingdom."

Some people are born with a fully developed spiritual consciousness and some with a measure of it, but most people have to cultivate it. The spiritual literature the student reads, the spiritual lectures he hears, the spiritual companionship along the way— all these help to lift him up and resurrect him from the material concepts in which he is entombed. When he is in the company of the spiritually minded, he is above material sense; whereas the more he holds himself in the companionship of the materially

[1] John 14:27.

44

minded, the more he holds himself to the wheel of life—going round and round but getting nowhere.

Life Cannot be Entombed in the Body

There are certain principles of The Infinite Way which an advanced student should know and which will aid in freeing him from the wheel of life. One of the most important of these is the principle that we are not in the body. At this moment, that may not seem to be of too much importance, but sooner or later it will be realized that this is the ultimate and the deepest secret of life, and the one which produces the highest demonstration of spiritual living.

We do not live in our bodies, nor are we the body. For that reason, no one should ever make such a statement as, "I am ill," for *I* am never ill. The body may be ill, suffering and in torment, but not *I*— not *I*, for *I* am not in that body to be ill. *I* am nowhere around where the pain or discord is, because *I* do not inhabit this body.

When the first glimmer that you do not live in your body comes, it causes you to look yourself up and down, in and out, when you are in meditation, and ultimately it will bring you to the realization, "Certainly, *I* am not in these knees, in this stomach, in this chest, nor am *I* up here in the brain. I know that *I* am somewhere else."

Eventually you will begin to realize the nature of that word *I* and you will see that you have been finitizing the word *I*: You have been using it in a purely limited personal sense as if there were an "I" separate and apart from the *I* which is you, as if the *I* which is you were something separate

45

from the *I* which is my identity. The fact that some people are healthier than others and that some are wealthier than others is based on that very belief of a separate selfhood apart from the one infinite Selfhood which is God.

When you catch a tiny glimpse of the truth that life is not entombed in the body, you will understand the meaning of the Resurrection. It is true that Jesus was entombed, that is, confined in a tomb, just as today it appears that human beings are confined to their bodies. But when the tomb was opened, was Jesus there? No, he had risen. The Christ, the divine Self, could not be entombed: The Christ, your divine Self, cannot be entombed in a body, and some day the realization must come, "I am not entombed in a body; I never was entombed in a body. I live and move and have my being in God— not in the tomb of material concept. I abide in the word of God, and the word of God abides in me— not in the body."

I *Govern the Body*

There is no place in the body where the word of God can be hidden, and yet the commandment is to "abide in me" and to let "my words abide in you."[1] When the spiritual perception of that is achieved, you will be able to look at this body and understand:

I—the very I *upon which I have been meditating—was given dominion over this body.* I *was given dominion over everything on earth, beneath the earth, and above the earth.* I *have dominion over this body;* I *govern it;* I *feed it;* I

[1] John 15:7.

46

care for it. I take my body out of this world where it has been at the mercy of weather and climate, of food, and of calendars that testify to the passing of time. I take my body out of the carnal mind by realizing that this body is my precious possession, given me of the Father. I—not calendars, wind, or weather—was given charge over this body which has been entrusted to my care.

If we inherit some valued possession such as a diamond, a jade statue, or an oil painting, we frequently take better care of it than we do of our own body. Over such material things, we almost invariably exercise dominion; but, when it comes to the body, we seem to think that it can take care of itself. The truth is that the body must be cared for much more tenderly than any work of art, only in a different way. It is not cared for by fussing over it: It is cared for by a kind of divine indifference which stems from the realization that *I* govern the body and that this body is the possession of my spiritual being.

There is no need for a person to worry about any organ or function of his body any more than he normally would be concerned about his breathing, digestion, or elimination. All those things the *I* cares for unconsciously. Therefore, let *I* govern the entire body. How? By realizing ten, twelve, twenty times a day:

Thank You, Father, I am not in the body: I govern the body; I have dominion over the body; I, the very Spirit of the Lord God, is the principle and the law unto my body. Knowing that I am not in the body, but that I govern it, I give my body to my divine Self for Its government.

Once you understand *I* to be the governing and

47

maintaining principle of life and then accept the body as Its instrument, you can readily understand that the determining factor in what the body does or does not do is the *I*. *I* am the principle; *I* am the law unto the body—only *I*. And then you begin to realize that your body is just as immobile as this paper is—unless *I* am in charge. But when *I* am in charge, every member of the body—the whole body—responds.

Your body is more subject unto you than is your automobile which, even though it may be the most expensive and luxurious in all the world, stands motionless until some intelligence moves it. So it is with your body. Your body can do no more of itself than can your automobile. At this moment, if you are not alert, your body is responding to the weather, to the climate, to the food you eat, to the day of the month, or to how many years the calendar says it is since you were born. Your body is responding to influences outside of you over which you have no control, unless you have begun to perceive the nature of *I* and have taken hold of that body:

See here! No more wandering out here in a human world for you! You live in me, and I *govern you.* I *am not in the body: The body is in me and is subject to my government and control, just the same as my pocketbook is. My pocketbook does not find itself wandering all over the streets and doing what it wants to do. It remains completely under control. And so does my body remain under my control because I am not in the body:* I *am the law unto the body, and* I *have God-given dominion over the body.* I *am the substance of the form of my body.*

My body is the out-picturing of my state of consciousness,

48

and if my body is not looking as well as it should, or feeling as good as it should, it is out-picturing my state of consciousness, and it is my state of consciousness about which I must do something.

What can you do about your state of consciousness? Humanly nothing, but you can lift your consciousness by realizing that consciousness is *I*, and *I* is not a human being with limited vision or limited wisdom. *I* is the very offspring of God, God's own Selfhood expressing Itself individually. *I* is not human: *I* is divine. *I* does not have to control the body by conscious thinking or psychological beliefs. *I* left to Itself governs the body: *I* knew enough to form this body, therefore *I* knows enough to govern this body and maintain it and sustain it. My part is to realize the truth, and the truth is that to know Him aright is life eternal.

"Whom Say Ye That I Am?"

The way to an eternal and an immortal body is to know God aright. How can you do that? By discovering your true identity and learning who *I* is. Understand why the Master asked the question, "Whom do men say that I the Son of man am?"[1] and then asked, "Whom say ye that I am?"[2] Why did he rephrase his question and change it from "Whom do men say that I the Son of man am?" to "Whom say *ye* that I am?" except because he knew that there were bound to be two different answers? He knew that men would look at him and see him only as the young Jeshua whom they knew as the carpenter's son or as Mary's son or as a carpenter or

[1] Matthew 16:13.   [2] Matthew 16:15.

a Hebrew rabbi. But when he asked his disciples, "Whom say *ye*?" he expected an answer from an enlightened consciousness. And that answer was, "Thou art the Christ."[1]

Any human being in the world can learn to identify you by name, by your birth date or birthplace, by your nationality or race. But if you ask an illumined person what your identity is, he will respond, "I know thee who thou art: Thou art the Christ, the Son of the living God." Eventually every seeker comes to that place in consciousness where he knows his true identity and where he begins to realize, "I am not in this body: This body is mine, and I was given dominion over it."

You may have thought that this body is your Self, and, thereby, may have identified your Self with the body; but this body never was you—it was yours; it is yours. There could be no truth at all to immortality if this body were you. No, there must be something besides this body.

In higher moments of spiritual uplift, students may have the experience of either being about eighteen inches in back of their body and seeing their entire form, or they may find themselves standing right beside themselves, and then they know that, although their body may be standing there, in reality, *I*—the *I* of them—is standing here, there, and everywhere.

These are not unusual experiences. In fact, they are very common to the advanced student, but no advanced student would deliberately attempt to bring them about, because he would know that he

[1] Matthew 16:16.

could not succeed. Such experiences come to the student only through Grace, naturally and of their own accord, but it is almost certain that they will not come while the student is wholly absorbed in living a mortal, material kind of life. They will only happen in those moments when he is "absent from the body, and . . . present with the Lord,"[1] present with the Lord through his moments of meditation.

No student should try to leave his body; he should never try to make a demonstration of this nature, nor should he ever try to make an occult or spiritual demonstration of any nature, because to seek any such phenomena is a wrong desire. There is only one right desire in The Infinite Way and that is to know God: "And this is life eternal, that they might know thee the only true God."[2]

In seeking and searching to understand God, the nature of God as *I* was revealed to me, I learned that God cannot be revealed by such terms as "Mind," "Soul," "Spirit," "Truth," "Life," or "Love," because those are words out here separate and apart from the thinker, and God cannot be something separate and apart from the thinker. When you ponder that, you discover that the thinker is *I*, because *I* am doing the thinking.

The only word that describes God, and which is not objective to the thinker, is *I*. When you comprehend that, you have the secret of life—the secret of the Resurrection—because in the *I* that I am are my supply, my opportunity, and my talents. In the *I* that I am are the grace of God and the law of God.

[1] II Corinthians 5:8.   [2] John 17:3.

The *I* that I am is the embodiment, the fullness of the Godhead bodily. All this is embodied in the *I Am*.

All Good Is Embodied in the I *of Individual Being*

As this is discerned, you perceive that you need nothing from anyone out in the world. You can share with anyone and everyone, and they can share with you, but no one needs the other because each one is Self-complete in God:

I am Self-sufficient; I am Self-contained. "I and my Father are one,"[1] and all that the Father has is mine. That allness includes companionship, opportunity, art, gifts, talent, and supply unto eternity—an infinite amount of it, even to twelve baskets full left over. All of this is embodied in the I that I am which I demonstrate in proportion as I release everyone in the world, as I loose every person and let him go in the realization that we owe one another nothing, but to love one another. That is all.

Because "I and my Father are one," all that the Father has is mine; and therefore, I am not dependent on "man, whose breath is in his nostrils."[2] I am not dependent on the good will of anybody. I and the Father are one, and that oneness makes it possible for me to share abundantly and infinitely with all.

In proportion as you know this truth, it sets you free to share with anyone you like, in your family or out of your family, as abundantly as you wish to share, with no restrictions and with no limitations. It really makes no difference whether those with whom you share deserve it or not. It is your good pleasure to share, just as it is my good pleasure to

1 John 10:30.   2 Isaiah 2:22.

share this message that has unfolded in my life and my joy to carry it around the world. What reaction it sets up in those who hear it is their demonstration. Those who recognize that they are being offered the "pearl of great price"[1] benefit by it. Those who do not miss it for the time being, until they hear it somewhere else at some other time.

When you understand *I*, you will understand that everything is embodied in that *I* which I am and which you are—even this message of truth. If this message were not embedded and embodied in my consciousness, how could it flow out from me to you? Do you see that? It is of God, but because it is of God, it must be embodied within me and within you, for *I* and the Father are one. Therefore, anything at all that you can conceive of as being in and of the Godhead, you must begin to understand is likewise in you.

If you have been expecting your good to come to you, you have missed the way. You must give up all desire for good to come to you; and instead of such vain desires, you must open out a way for good to escape from you, because you embody within you every bit of truth, life, love, bread, wine, and water, even the power of resurrection—everything is embodied within you because it is embodied in God, and *I* and the Father are one.

"The earth is the Lord's, and the fulness thereof,"[2] but all that the Father has is ours because of our relationship of oneness with the Father. Sometimes it is impossible to see how each one of us can embody all of the Godhead, but it becomes very simple to

[1] Matthew 13:46.   [2] Psalm 24:1.

understand this point if we consider the subject of morality, honesty, integrity, or loyalty. Can morality or loyalty be divided and each one of us embody five percent of morality or loyalty? No, each of us claims for himself the wholeness because that is the nature of loyalty and morality. These are qualities of God; therefore, they are equally ours because of our relationship of heir with Christ in God to all the heavenly riches.

"Ah," but you say, "certainly those qualities are spiritual, but I am not talking about them; I am talking about supply." When you say that, you indicate that you are thinking of supply as material and of those other things as spiritual. Do not make that mistake. Supply is as spiritual as loyalty, morality, or honesty, because supply is Spirit. It is the law of God working in you. The dollar bill and the pound sterling are not supply: They are forms of supply, just as this body is not *I*, but the form of me. *I* am separate from the form, and so supply is separate from any dollars or pounds I may possess.

You are the law and the substance unto your supply, and your pounds or dollars are but the outward expression of that supply. The more you realize that you embody the fulness of the Godhead, that "the earth is the Lord's, and the fulness thereof," and that all that the Father has is yours, the more dollars you will have to share with others, and the more you will have left over. But as long as you think that pounds or dollars mean supply or that they are your personal possession, you shut yourself off from supply.

The earth, which is the Lord's and the fulness thereof,

is mine—infinitely mine—but only because "I and my Father are one." It is my oneness with God which constitutes my oneness with all spiritual being. As myself alone, I would be as the branch that is cut off and withereth, but by virtue of my oneness with God, the infinity of the God-life is mine.

Oneness is the truth of being, but if you are to witness your own resurrection above lack and limitation, that oneness must be realized. Whether the need is for a truth or a dollar bill, a hotel or an airplane reservation, always turn within for its fulfillment. Never do I, and never should you, make a human move without first turning within. Waking in the morning, my very first act is to meditate and to continue that process of turning within, thirty, forty, and fifty times, during the day and night, because I of myself know nothing, I of myself am nothing, and I of my own self have nothing. Whatever I have or whatever I express is only by virtue of my oneness with God. Therefore, I must turn to that Source which is not within my body, but which is Itself the Within-ness, within consciousness. Then whatever the next need is, I am made aware of it and of its manner of fulfillment.

"Not my will, but thine, be done"[1] is nothing but words unless it is carried out by actions, and this can never be done unless there are countless periods of meditation during the day and night to find out what the will of the Father is. This constant turning within for guidance, direction, and fulfillment dispels material sense and reveals the risen Christ.

The Resurrection, properly understood, shows us

[1] Luke 22:42.

that the imprisoned Christ, which seems to be locked up in this tomb of human experience and in this human body, really is not there at all. When spiritual illumination is achieved, it is discovered that *I* never was confined to a body or to an environment, because *I* am infinite, unlimited, divine Consciousness.

*   *   *

TRANSCENDENTAL CONSCIOUSNESS

Students on the spiritual path are continuously condemning themselves because they do not have spiritual experiences or do not hear the still small voice or because they do not feel that inner peace which passeth understanding. Often they feel that if they have been on the Path three years, or five or ten, and in all that time have not had any significant spiritual experience, that this way is not for them, or that perhaps those who claim to have had those experiences actually have only experienced their own imagination.

All of this doubt, uncertainty, lack of spiritual awareness, or even self-condemnation stems from the fact that the student does not realize that a human being with the ordinary materialistic human consciousness cannot have this experience. The young student seeking to know God or to have spiritual experiences, or inner illumination, will have to learn that, before such experiences can come to him, it is necessary that he have a developed spiritual consciousness, the Soul-faculties or power of spiritual discernment, through which these experiences can come.

From the beginning of his study, then, the student should be concerned not so much with attaining the God-experience, with gaining an inner light or seeing a vision, but rather with developing the consciousness through which such experiences come. This consciousness is developed by reading the writings and the revelations of the spiritually illumined men and women of all time. This, of course, requires discrimination as to what constitutes the illumined literature of the world, since much that passes for such writings represents but an intellectual repetition or a personal interpretation and personal version of experiences the spiritually illumined have actually had.

Even in the reading of the scriptures of the world, it is necessary to pray to be spiritually guided in this reading so as to be led to that which is the result of illumination, and not that which represents thoughts and opinions, and to pray before such reading so that the spiritual interpretation of the scripture may be given the student, rather than its literal meaning which often is of little or no value to those seeking illumination. He should ask for guidance and direction and, above all things, for understanding in his reading, and then let that asking be followed by a few moments of complete silence to let the Spirit take hold. He should read slowly, attentively, and ponder at each step the words that are being read, going back again and again, if necessary, because it is not the quantity of material that is read that is the determining factor, but the degree of unfoldment which comes forth from the reading. Often one sentence or one paragraph is sufficient for this purpose. The student should not attempt to see how much material can be read, but rather how much light and how much understanding can be received from each sentence or paragraph that is read. In this way, spiritual discernment is developed.

Often from such reading one particular statement or passage will stand out above all the others, and as you close your book, you should let this passage remain consciously within you. Ponder it, repeat it, think upon it, because this passage is a seed of truth which is now being planted within you, and then after you have ceased thinking about it, that seed begins to germinate and eventually takes root, later bearing spiritual fruitage in the form of understanding, wisdom, guidance, and the spiritual experience itself.

Every time you hear a message of truth, whether in lectures, class, or on tape recordings, the word of God is also being planted within you as a seed, or as a dozen seeds, and out of these even one, springing up into life, will be sufficient for every purpose. Your periods of meditation, in which you contemplate some passage of truth, ponder it, think upon it, and then finally settle into an inner stillness and let the Spirit bear witness with your spirit, also develop your Soul-faculties.

Do you see now that your work is not attempting to reach God or to have spiritual experiences, but rather to develop the faculties necessary to receiving the spiritual light and to attaining spiritual consciousness and, thereby, gaining dominion.

This, of course, is written especially for those of you who receive the Infinite Way monthly *Letter*, and most of you already have a considerable metaphysical and spiritual background. From the very beginning of your turning to a metaphysical or spiritual approach to life, you have been developing your inner faculties, and from this point onward, your progress should be more rapid because you now consciously know what you are doing and you know better how to do it. Probably never before have you realized what you were doing, why you were doing it, or even knew an orderly and systematic way of accomplishing it, but in the message of The Infinite Way all this is provided.

With this daily devotion to your reading the Word, hearing the Word, and meditating upon the Word, I give you my assurance that the spiritual experiences will come to you of their own accord, because it is inevitable that these experiences come once the latent spiritual capacities are aroused. Then, to those ready for the experience, personal contact with the spiritually illumined will provide the greatest impetus to spiritual unfoldment and illumination. You need only think back upon the effect on their disciples of such masters as Gautama, the Buddha; or Jesus, the Christ; or Jacob Boehme to understand what I mean. Or perhaps you may have met someone who came under the influence of the individual consciousness of Vivekananda, Maharshi, Walt Whitman, Mary Baker Eddy, or Emmett Fox. And of course the effect on human consciousness of such illumined Souls as Krishnamurti, Henry Thomas Hamblin, and others too numerous to mention is well known. Be assured of this, that whenever you come in contact with an

59

illumined Soul, some measure of illumination is brought to you.

Always remember that every step of your journey on the spiritual path should be preceded by prayer. Pray for light, for discernment, for judgment, for awakening, and then there will be a message for you in every bit of inspired literature that you read or from every illumined Soul whom you meet.

This leads us, naturally, to a question that is often asked by students, "Why, since I have been studying truth so long, can I not heal others?" or, "Why can I not meet the problems of my family?" The answer is that although you may have read truth and heard truth for a considerable period of time, you have not practiced it sufficiently to bring about the development of your spiritual consciousness. Remember, it is not the statements that you know or that you can repeat that do the healing work. These are but preparations. The healing of mind and body and of human relationships is accomplished only through what is called spiritual consciousness, Christ-consciousness, or the spiritual nature of the individual. The study of the correct letter of truth, the pondering of scriptural statements, the contemplation of the word of God, the meditations—all these develop the spiritual nature which, in its turn, produces healings in human affairs. When this consciousness is realized, one has entered the fourth dimension of life, and he now beholds the world in an entirely different way than the human mind can perceive.

On the ordinary plane of life, you have two powers, good and evil, and always you are striving through the power of good to overcome evil. This is true not only on the physical plane but on the mental plane as well. Only upon attaining spiritual consciousness are you in the realm of one power, and there both the power of good and the power of evil are swallowed up in the power of God.

ACROSS THE DESK

The Infinite Way reveals that our ultimate destiny is conscious union with God. From the beginning, even "before Abraham was . . . I and my Father are one," indivisible and inseparable, harmonious and complete, but century after century of human living has set up a sense of separation, as that of a branch cut off from the tree. Now, having been led to the spiritual path, we seek conscious realization of our spiritual relationship with God.

Through The Infinite Way, the many steps to be taken by each student leading to this attainment are revealed. Since God-realization is an individual affair, *your* demonstration will be at whatever level *you* determine it shall be. In the degree that you study, ponder, meditate, and practice Infinite Way principles, will you progress toward your goal. In the degree that you abstain from human cares, human living, and human concerns, and to the extent that you immerse yourself in the Writings and in meditation, in that degree, will your consciousness develop, ripen, and deepen spiritually. This does not bring about a disregard of family obligations or civic duties. On the contrary, your spiritual realizations bring out greater harmony in these experiences and activities.

Often students accept the belief that some person, some relationship, or some family situation can limit the degree of attainment, or that lack of adequate finances can hinder them. The truth is that no one can block your unfoldment but you yourself. If you are determined to attain God-realization, you will devote as many hours to study, meditation, and the practice of the principles as may be necessary even if these hours extend far into the night or begin in the early hours of dawn.

There are twenty-four hours in every day. How will you allocate these? To what purpose will you dedicate these hours and your efforts? With what cares or chores can you dispense? What unnecessary reading can you lay aside for the few years ahead of you? What things that might hinder your progress can you forgo? How much time devoted to radio, television, and moving pictures can you omit from your schedule? You alone determine that. You are the master of your time, your body, and your attention.

The Infinite Way, recognizing that the spiritual urge must come from within and that it will be different with each student, does not prescribe a set amount of reading, study, or meditation, and it demands no obedience to rules or regulations, to modes or methods. There is a "pearl of great price," and it is yours—if you so desire. Furthermore, attaining it, the added things of health, joy, success, peace, and happiness will be yours, plus the opportunity to share your "pearl" with those who also seek.

During December and January, many students

came to Hawaii, and we have had beautiful experiences at Halekou—hours of inspiration, meditation, and instruction, parts of which were recorded on two new Halekou Group tapes. Early in January, we were on the Island of Maui for a visit with our students there, where I wish all of you might have joined us for our Chinese dinner and for a Japanese dinner. The four talks given to the students on Maui were also recorded on two new Maui Advanced tapes.

Once more I have been invited to give the Maundy Thursday and Easter Sunday talks for the Scottish Rite, Thirty-second Degree Masonic work. As the Master washed the feet of his disciples and as the Queen of England symbolically performs that same rite on Maundy Thursday, so do we express our humility and devotion by our service to the poor in spirit—to those who seek the riches of the Spirit. Easter Sunday reveals the Resurrection, a rising from the tomb of the body into that consciousness which is never circumscribed by physical limitations or human concepts.

The unfoldment, which began in Holland, continues to flow, and so I remain quietly at home until instructions come to travel.

SPIRITUAL POWER IN HUMAN AFFAIRS

Address delivered at Zeist, Holland, August 29, 1958

GOOD morning, Friends! Good morning, and a very good morning, too. To speak to you about spiritual power in human affairs becomes a very simple matter if, to begin with, we understand how spiritual power operates and how it is brought into human experience.

You have heard the chairman of this meeting quote a statement from Saint Augustine to the effect that God cares for every individual, for every little bit of God's creation. Rightly understood, this passage is the truth, but a misunderstanding of it has made it impossible for the church to perform its function on earth and extend to man the spiritual powers which are his birthright. Such a statement as that of Saint Augustine's is in keeping with many biblical promises of God's grace to His creation which are statements of truth provable and demonstrable in our daily experience.

The Ninety-first Psalm states that if you dwell in the secret place of the most High, many of the evils of human experience will not come nigh your dwelling place. But may I point out to you that it says, "A thousand shall fall at thy side, and ten thousand at thy right hand."[1] That does not indicate that God cares for every human being on the face of the earth, for He very clearly tells us of the thousand on the left and the ten thousand on the right who will fall into the snare and the pit.

If you go from the Old Testament to the New, you will find the same message presented in the fifteenth chapter of John. It is unfortunate that this has been overlooked, because if the fifteenth chapter of John were correctly understood, interpreted, and lived, today there would be no wars or threats of wars, no famine, no pestilence, no sin, and no disease. In this chapter, the Master points out that if you abide in this Word and let this Word abide in you, you will bear fruit richly; but if you do not abide in this Word, if you do not let this Word abide in you, you will be as a branch of a tree that is cut off and withereth. This does not indicate that God cares equally for all. No, God cares only for those who dwell in the secret place of the most High or for those who abide in the Word and let the Word abide in them.

Whether you turn to Hebrew Scripture or to Christian Scripture, and, of course, if we had the time, we could go back into Oriental Scripture, you will find this same teaching that salvation, healing, protection, and care are given only to those who abide in the Word. "Thou wilt keep him in perfect peace, whose mind is stayed on thee"[2]—stayed on Thee, not for an hour on Sunday, not merely at Easter time or Christmas time, but *stayed on Thee*. "In all thy ways acknowledge him, and he shall

[1] Psalm 91:7.　　[2] Isaiah 26:3.

direct thy paths."[1] Acknowledge Him in all your ways, from waking in the morning to sleeping at night; express gratitude for the table that is set before you in the wilderness; acknowledge God as the very life and intelligence of your being, that which gives you all that you can offer to the world, that which gives the world its art, literature, poetry, science, wisdom, intelligence, guidance, and strength. "In quietness and in confidence shall be your strength,"[2] not a quietness or confidence or faith in mankind, but a faith in a divine Presence that is always present when one abides in the Word and lets the Word abide in him.

Paul later said: "Pray without ceasing."[3] It is sometimes believed that in this busy twentieth century world it is impossible to pray without ceasing, but I say to you from the experience many thousands of people have had that this is not true. It is possible to pray without ceasing. It is possible to awaken in the morning and instantly give recognition to the fact that only by the grace of God are we alive and awake; it is possible at breakfast time to acknowlege that but for the grace of God there would be no food in the ground, no cattle on a thousand hills, and that all this is maintained and sustained from its creation by an invisible Presence and Power which mankind has forgotten. As you enter your place of business, you can realize that the Presence has gone before you to make the crooked places straight and to prepare the place for you. Throughout the day and throughout the night, occasions arise in which any one of us, every one of

[1] Proverbs 3:6.   [2] Isaiah 30:15.   [3] I Thessalonians 5:17.

66

us, may find it possible, if the desire is there, to acknowledge an invisible Power, even in the presence of the visible.

Evolving Concepts of God and Prayer

In ancient days, before man created a God, whom he has ever since ignorantly worshiped, he found life a difficult matter. Sometimes there was too much rain, and this destroyed his food; sometimes there was not enough rain, and that destroyed his food; and sometimes neighboring tribes raided his home, destroying his property, killing the men and kidnaping the women and children. In so many ways, living was such a difficult matter you could almost imagine it was the twentieth century! Probably under such circumstances, the idea was born that perhaps man cannot meet all the problems of human existence by himself, so he sought to find a supernatural power or a supernatural being, someone or something which could do for him that which he could not do for himself.

And so began the search for that which later was called God. Now, as you know, not only one God was found, but many gods—a god for the weather, a god for fertility, a god of the sun, of the moon, and of the stars—gods, gods, gods many. There were gods for this and gods for that; and, of course, these gods and later the one God did not always function the way God was expected to function.

The day eventually came—perhaps in India— when someone with great vision discovered that there were not gods many: There was only one God. This teaching of monotheism, the worship of one

67

God, spread from India to Egypt, where it was accepted by King Amenhotep IV who ordered that all the gods, their temples, symbols, and statues be destroyed, so that the one God could be worshipped. Those of you who have had any experience at all in weaning man away from his false concepts of God must know how impossible King Amenhotep's task was, and because of that, in a very few years, he was overthrown, deposed, and he fled.

Abraham, who later became known as the father of the Hebrews, also set up the worship of one God, founding a new religion which became the Hebrew faith. This one God had all the virtues of the many gods, and so it was that the belief perpetuated itself that man could pray to this God for favors: "Please destroy my enemies so that I can be at peace." It was believed that men could pray to this God and have Him do their will, not only that, but tell God what day in the week it should be done. In other words, this fantastic idea of praying to a God to do man's will continued with the one God much in the same way as with many gods. The only change was that instead of praying to many gods they prayed to one, but they prayed to this one God for the same things and for the same reasons that they had prayed to the many.

I do not have to recount for you the years of wandering of the Hebrews across the Holy Lands from the time of Abraham to the days of Jesus Christ, of the many times when they found temporary peace and prosperity only to be plunged into more wars, more slavery, and more lack from which they were redeemed by some great prophet and brought into harmony, wholeness, and joy, only to fall again by the wayside. Throughout all those centuries, it was not learned that God does not answer the prayers of mortals, that God is not interested in human welfare, nor does God protect human society as human society is constituted.

It is for this reason that, even though two thousand years have elapsed since prayer and an approach to the one true God were properly taught, man still finds himself in the position of witnessing, in World War I, World War II, and the Korean War, men gathering together in churches to pray to God for the success of their side, to pray to God to kill all their enemies but not their own boys; men sending chaplains to war to pray for their side that they may be uninjured, not sick and not dead, while they send their own sons to wipe out the enemy, an enemy who has ministers of the same churches praying for this very same thing. This may not seem incongruous to you, but if you could look out with spiritual eyes at the lamentable sight of one man praying for the destruction of another, you would humbly sink to your knees, begging forgiveness that you might ever have been guilty of asking God to give you protection at the expense of a fellow being.

Prayer today is about on the same level, on the whole, as it was in pagan days when men prayed for crops and for cattle to be abundant, when they even prayed for prosperity, when they prayed for protection for their personal selves and prayed for the destruction of their enemy. The pagans did that, but two thousand years ago we were taught that you must not pray for yourself, for what you shall eat or for what you shall drink or wherewithal you shall be clothed. You must seek only the kingdom of God, God who knows your need and whose good pleasure it is to give you the kingdom, and then all of these things will be added. It is a strange thing that men still can meet in churches to pray for victory for their side when one, whom we know to be an authority, clearly stated that it profiteth you nothing to pray for your friends. You must pray for your enemies that you may be children of God.

A Concept of God Cannot Answer Prayer

As children of God, you are heirs of God, joint-heirs to all the heavenly riches. But how do you become children of God? By taking no thought for your life, by taking no thought for what you shall eat, or what you shall drink, or wherewithal you shall be clothed; by seeking only the kingdom of God and His righteousness and letting all these things be added unto you; by praying for those who persecute you and despitefully use you; by praying for the enemy, not for the allies, but for the enemy—not praying that the enemy succeeds in overcoming you, but praying that the enemy's mind, heart, and soul be opened to the grace of God, to divine leading, to divine Grace. Pray that their sins be forgiven them, not that they be punished, but that they be forgiven so that this grace of God can enter into them and regenerate them.

Prayer can never be successfully carried on as long as we have in our heart animosity, jealousy, envy, hate, or destructive feelings towards another fellow being. Scripture states specifically that if you go to the altar to pray and there remember that any man has aught against you, get up and leave the altar, first make peace with your fellow man, and then return to the altar and pray. Then you will find that your prayers are fulfilled.

How do we make this peace? We cannot walk around the world extending our hands to the people in the north, south, east, or west, who at the moment may be our enemies, but we can get up from the altar and go into a quiet spot in our own home and there pray the prayer of forgiveness:

Father, forgive them; they do not know what they do. Father, open the eyes and the minds and the hearts and the souls of mankind, whether on our side of the border or on the other, whether on our side of the color line or on the other. Open the minds and the hearts and the souls of mankind to Thy presence and to Thy grace.

Then go back to the altar and see how effective prayer can be.

At sixteen and a half years of age, it was my good fortune to be sent to Europe from the United States on business, and except during the actual war years, I have been travelling the world ever since. And so it has been my joy and privilege to know men, women, and children in all countries, of all religious faiths, and of all colors.

As far back as 1909, World War I was imminent. In the fall of that year, the English Navy and the German Navy were lined up against each other in the North Sea ready to fight, but wiser heads prevailed, and war did not come until 1914. But those of us who travelled Europe on business knew from 1909 on that War could happen any month.

In those earlier years of my travels, I often wondered at the amount of sin, disease, and discord that existed in the world, for it existed then as it does now.

These things puzzle a young man. Why should such things be? And, certainly, travelling cities like Paris, London, Berlin, and Vienna, where every visitor quickly gets to know the night spots of the world, it is impossible for a youngster not to wonder. The great hospitals were pointed out and the sanitoriums, and again the thought came, "Why? Why on every corner a church and yet in every corner sin, disease, death, limitation, fear, discord, and inharmony? Why?" And then I visited churches and watched people at prayer, at worship: They were sincere, they were honest, they were really there in the hope that God's grace would reach them, and they were willing for it to reach all mankind; they placed no limits.

The average person is not a bad person. When you consider the good will of men of every nation and religion, and yet witness their discords and inharmonies, you are puzzled, you wonder, and ultimately the question may come to you as it did to me, "Why is not prayer answered?" I know that people delude themselves into believing that prayers are answered. Even men who are very intelligent, wise, and great in their own fields, when it comes to a matter of religion, can be so hypnotized as to believe all the mythology that is presented to them under the guise of religion. I am thinking in particular of a physician in the United States who is undoubtedly distinguished in his field. If anyone were to go to him and announce that he had found a remedy for a horrible disease and that he should experiment with it on 100,000 cases to see if it did not have therapeutic value; and if he tried it on the 100,000 cases and discovered that only fifteen of the 100,000 were healed, he would probably say that he was afraid the remedy was a failure and that he would not want to recommend it or trust it. But this same person decided to investigate faith-healing and discovered that out of 100,000 people praying to God, fifteen of them were healed. He then wrote a book and stated that he knew that God answers prayer. That may not seem strange to you, but it does to me. If there were fifteen healings, there were fifteen reasons why these people received healing, fifteen cases of people who for one reason or another rose out of their human selves enough to find healing. Be assured that if God were doing the healing the figure would have been reversed with 99,985 healed and fifteen not healed.

So it is that if you look at this world objectively, you have to acknowledge that people have been praying for peace since before Abraham's time, and they have not yet achieved it. Mothers have been praying for the health of their babies and their children, and they still become sick and die until some material means saves them. God does not. You must acknowledge how many women have prayed and prayed and prayed for their men folk only to see the men folk go the way of all flesh. You must know that prayer as it is generally understood is ineffective. The question is, "Why?"

Now when you come back to the Bible or the scriptures of any people, you will learn that there is one great error in man's calculations, one great fallacy in his prayers. He is praying with his mind to a human concept of God, and a concept of God cannot answer prayer, even if it is a good concept. The human mind with all its great powers can never reach God. Paul saw this so clearly that he could say that the things of God are foolishness to man. As a matter of fact, the mind of man is enmity against God, cannot please God, and cannot come under the law of God. This has all been forgotten except in the experience of the few dozen mystics of the world who have become known, although there may be some hundreds of mystics who have never become known. The mystics of the world know this secret and always have. Therefore, to the extent of their understanding, their prayers are answered, because they do the one thing that mankind has not been taught to do: *They make direct contact with God.*

When you think of God as infinite Intelligence and divine Love, when you think of God as something more than the superhuman being about which most people are taught, when you think of God as the creative Principle of all that is, you begin to understand how foolish it is to pray to God in the sense of trying to tell God what you or I would like, and especially when we would like it, or as is sometimes taught now, "Do not pray for a Ford; it is just as easy to pray for a Cadillac and get it." Such forms of prayer, in which man attempts to enlighten God, to tell God what things he has need of and when he would like them, are foolishness. The things of God certainly are foolishness to man, and the things of man must be foolishness with God.

74

There is no God unless there is an infinite intelligence, and this God does not need to be enlightened by man. There is no God unless God is divine love, infinite, impersonal love, and this God is not withholding anything and, therefore, need not be asked for anything.

The One Essential Is Contact with God

One thing only is needed—contact with God. And God can only be contacted where God is—within you. The Master warned us to worship no longer in holy mountains or in temples. As a matter of fact, he said that you must not pray where you can be seen of men, but enter into the sanctuary of your being, close the door, and, where men cannot witness your praying, the Father that seeth in secret will reward you openly. This we violate every day of the week, as you know. You must do your alms in secret, not where man can see, not where man can know the size of your check, or to whom you sent it; but do your alms where man can never become aware of them because there is One who knows, the Infinite Invisible that is within the consciousness of every individual on the face of the globe. This Infinite Invisible which knows us in our inner being comes forth into expression in proportion to our own integrity.

The whole subject of spiritual power in human affairs challenged my attention many, many years ago, and my search for the answer resulted in the actual experience of contact with God. Perhaps I am a little bit slower of perception than most people because it took me thirteen years to attain it while I can often help students to attain it in one year. *But it can be attained.* When it is attained, there is no such thing as unanswered prayer, but by that time prayer has taken on a different form: Prayer now has no words and no thoughts. Prayer is an entering into God's presence with the realization that this infinite, creative Principle which has made everything from a blade of grass to the stars in the heavens fills our lands with food, our barns with crops or cattle, our sea with fish, our air with birds; this all-knowing infinite Intelligence, which is a divine Love, flows into expression in ways that we know not of.

It is only a few months ago that I heard of this town, this group of people, and this work in which you are engaged; and so you can see how fantastic it would have been for me to try to sit down and pray to be invited to speak here. How nonsensical to approach God in any such way! And yet sitting in that complete silence, knowing and realizing that this spiritual impulse within me governs and guides every movement of my experience—the activity of my heart, the strength of my muscles, and that which comes forth from the mind—that every moment It is maintaining and sustaining me where I can best fulfill God's purpose, step by step, I am led here today, to Canada next month, to South Africa next year, a total of some 53,000 miles from Australia to here and back again, and all this without taking thought, without planning, without even providing the means, but only through the contact which is itself an inner grace.

I hope that you can feel something of what I am trying to say because this represents thirty years of my life, and I am trying to impart it in sixty minutes, a difficult task. However, you do not necessarily have to hear the words that I am saying; you do not even have to believe them; you do not have to understand them, if only you can *feel* that I am trying to say to you that there is an invisible Something about which Lao-tze said more than 2500 years ago, "If you can name it, it is not that." Do not try to form concepts of what this infinite Intelligence, this divine Love, is because the mind of man cannot grasp it; it can only feel and know that *God is*. A Hebrew mystic of 1100 A.D. wrote that if you say that God is love or God is intelligence or God is omnipresent or God is good, you are saying no more than if you had just said: God is.

And what I am trying to say to you is that we cannot grasp God with our minds; but with our feelings, we can know that God is and that His grace is our sufficiency. What His grace is I cannot outline, whether it is to be a Ford, a Cadillac, or no car at all, to be in Holland or in South Africa, or to eat well or poorly on any given day. That is not my function. My function is to let God's grace flow through me to the world. I must hold no man in condemnation, even for his sins, recognizing that his sins are not really sins, but only errors of understanding. The Master could forgive even Judas Iscariot, knowing that Judas probably was not responsible for having been born with too great an ambition for the worldly things of life. The Master could not condemn Peter, realizing that self-preservation is the first law of human nature and that even spiritual people sometimes become so unspiritual that they want to preserve their lives.

When we look at mankind in that same way, realizing that the thief is not stealing because he is a sinner, but because at that moment he has no knowledge of the law of supply and at the moment it seems to him his only way out, we can forgive. When we know that a sinner is acting through ignorance, we do not hold him in condemnation. It is not necessary that people live by the sweat of their brow, nor that they bring forth children in pain. That merely represents their degree of ignorance of spiritual law and of spiritual life.

The Belief in Two Powers Is the One Evil

In the beginning Adam and Eve dwelt in Eden, in spiritual harmony and grace, with no human problems; but something happened in their lives which forever changed the course of human events. How it happened we do not know, but they came to accept two powers—the belief that there is good and evil. Thereby, they brought upon themselves and all of us the horrors of human existence because as long as this belief in two powers exists there will be warfare, strife, and struggle. In early days, the tribes that had bows and arrows could always overcome those which had none; later those with pistols overcame those with bows and arrows; still later machine guns supplanted rifles; and now nuclear fission has become the decisive factor in modern warfare. Those with the greatest material power have always been able to overcome those with less material power. This will always be, as long as men live by the code of two powers. Always the greater power will destroy the lesser power; always one will destroy the other.

Whether it is physical power or mental, as long as you accept two powers you will have one consuming the other, one battling the other; and it is for this reason that it can safely be said that peace will never come on earth through human means—by means of armaments or by means of peace treaties and international agreements. No government is going to sign any agreement detrimental to itself unless the power against it is greater than its own. Regardless of who signs a contract it will not be fulfilled for any longer period of time than it suits the purpose of that particular government. Certainly, agreements have not been kept in your time or mine or before that.

Is there then no hope for mankind? Of course there is. It is the hope that was given 2000 years ago when Jesus told us that there is only one power, and that every other so-called power is only power while it is accepted by the mind of man. And so this healer could command the crippled man to take up his bed and walk because there is no power but God. He could walk up to a blind man and heal him with nothing but spittle—and certainly nobody believes that there is power in spittle. In other words, every demonstration of healing by the great Master was performed upon the basis that there is no power in the condition.

Attaining Success in Spiritual Healing

Today there is a spiritual healing movement around this world, not merely that of Christian Science or Unity, but an ever broadening, spiritual healing ministry. Much of it is not successful, but that is not the fault of the principle. It is the fault of those who practice spiritual healing who do not know the principle and who have not properly prepared themselves for the healing ministry. There are too many among those who call themselves spiritual healers who believe that a few weeks, a few months, or even a few years of study entitle them to go out and heal spiritually. Physicians spend from seven to ten years in universities and hospitals before they are granted a license to practice. Spiritual healing requires an equal, if not greater, amount of preparation, dedication, and consecration.

Whatever degree of success in spiritual healing is attained, is attained on the basis that all power is vested in the Infinite Invisible which some people call God, others Consciousness, and still others by a different name. The name is of no importance because no name is correct; but God, the creative Principle of the universe, the maintaining and sustaining Principle of the universe, is power and, in reality, It is the only power there is. When one makes contact with that Power, sin, false appetite, disease, poverty, hate, envy, jealousy, and wars disappear out of the consciousness of the individual. When once this invisible Power is contacted, the limitations and discords of this world are removed. It was the recognition of this one and only Power which enabled Jesus to say to Pilate, the greatest temporal power of that day, "Thou couldest have no power at all against me, except it were given thee from above."[1]

[1] John 19:11.

Preparation for the experience of that Power comes through following the Master's teaching on the subject of prayer: first of all, purging ourselves of the animosities that ordinarily beset the human being; secondly, learning specifically to pray that the sins of mankind be forgiven them, that their ignorance be wiped away, and that the grace of God open consciousness to His presence, learning to live without a sense of condemnation towards those who are not yet awakened to some measure of the truth of being, learning never to pray for anything for ourselves or another, and letting prayer be this conscious union in which the all-knowing Intelligence and the divine Love are permitted to govern us—not our will be done, but Thine.

It is only because I have had the privilege for many years of saying these things to people in many different countries and have witnessed the fruits of this teaching that I know that it is possible of accomplishment. Those who abide in the Word—in this Word which reveals God's infinite nature, God's infinite intelligence, God's love—those who abide in this and acknowledge God as the Source of their being, will bear fruit richly. Peace cannot come to this world until it comes to you and to me individually. It is by my experience that my friends, my public, my students, and my readers judge me; and it is by your experience that members of your family, of your neighborhood, and of your community judge you. When you and I can show forth a greater sense of health, vitality, youth, and fewer fears and worries about supply, then we are demonstrating what the Master meant when he said: "My peace I give unto you: not as the world giveth, give I unto you"[1]—not name or fame of fortune, but *My peace*, the peace that will never pass away, the peace that the human world will never understand. When you and I can demonstrate that peace in our experience, one person here, another there, catches it; invisibly they catch it and they are led to follow some particular path which will lead them to God-realization. There is no one path that will lead all men to God or to their peace. Because God Itself is infinite being, there must be infinite paths for men to follow to find themselves home in God, under the grace of God.

Remember that the human race is not under the law of God and is not protected by it, supported by it, or supplied by it, but only individual you and I are, as we rise above our mortal selfhood by not responding to this world's hates and fears, and ultimately come to that place where we are the children of God, "if so be that the Spirit of God dwell"[2] in us. When we come to that point, we have meat the world knows not of; we do not have to compete for it, fight for it, or battle for it. We have spiritual Grace. We do not need man: We have the grace of God, established in us from the beginning. It is only necessary to awaken and become aware of that Grace.

It is not easy of accomplishment, but it is far better than living this worrisome life, always fearing for what tomorrow will bring. It is true that spiritual man will some day pass from this scene even as will the unspiritual, but he will not fear that transition;

<hr />

[1] John 14:27.   [2] Romans 8:9.

he will not think of it as death or extinction: He will recognize it for what it truly is, a passing from grace to grace, a passing from one experience of life to another. Those who prepare themselves for the experience of God's grace go from glory to glory.

ACROSS THE DESK

Daily we are being made aware of the dangers threatening the world: the danger of war; the danger of being taken over by Communistic leaders; and now the impending danger of a coalition of an aggressive and militant ecclesiasticism and the more radical elements of our political and economic life, which would end democracy as it has been known in this country and would deprive us of self-government. These are the major dangers threatening our world, and no one in public life has given us an answer to these problems, or a solution to them. The world continues to pray to its God, and no answer come forth.

Scripture teaches that all manner of evil may encompass the world, but these evils will not "come nigh *thy* dwelling" place. Why will thy dwelling place be safe? And the answer is "because thou hast made the Lord, which is my refuge, even the most High, thy habitation"; because we do not look "to might or to power" for our safety or security; because we do not look to "man, whose breath is in his nostrils" for peace, joy, or freedom. We have learned to acknowledge Him in all our ways and to trust not in our own, or any man's, understanding. Our trust is in a God who neither gives nor withholds, a God who eternally *is* "closer . . . than breathing."

Students of The Infinite Way, have faith that "ye shall not need to fight," that the armies and weapons of the alien are not power, but merely the "arm of flesh." *Resist the temptation to* fear or to battle by abiding in the scriptural assurance that "in quietness and in confidence shall be your strength."

GOD-REALIZATION DISSOLVES MATERIAL SENSE

THE human world is stumbling from one form of error into another, seldom if ever able to extricate itself from the web of its own weaving, but always rushing onward toward destruction. Those of spiritual enlightenment, however, who understand the nature of error will no longer battle or struggle against it; they will no longer try to find a cause for it; and, what is more important, they will no longer attempt to find a cure for it, because they will preceive that it is but the material and mental concept of the universe that is destroying man. It is not a material universe—there isn't one: It is the material concept and material sense of the universe that man entertains which is his destruction.

Material sense always operates through the word "I." It never appears in any form other than "I": "I need this"; "I require that"; "I have this"; or, "I do not have that"; "I long for this"; or, "I miss that"—always the word "I" appears negatively to hold us in its grasp. Or it may appear positively and say, "Oh, yes, I am healthy," or, "I am wealthy," and then sooner or later we find that we are not that at all. In other words, the personal sense of "I," claiming either to be something, have something, or do something, or the personal sense of "I," claiming that it cannot do something or does not have something—this personal sense of "I" constitutes material sense.

The personal sense of "I" is always under the necessity of acquiring, achieving, or attaining. Once this is perceived, it quickly appears that this personal sense is not a part of God's universe, never was, and never can be. We begin to understand that there is a spiritual Presence and a spiritual Power, and, in that perception, the personal sense of "I" is lost, and spiritual harmony begins to appear.

To all appearances, we remain the same as we have always been, except often with improved health of body or improved condition of purse. Outwardly, we are the same person, but inwardly we are now living by Grace instead of living by might or by power—by force and by energy—or instead of living by fear. Something has taken over in our experience, Something which goes before us to arrange the details of our existence, Something which acts as a cement in our relationships—a cement of love—a bond and a tie with all those with whom we come in contact.

What is it that dispels the material sense which appears as forms of sin, disease, lack, and limitation? What is it that dissolves all these appearances? What dissolves material sense? We may call It by any name we choose, but It is a Presence or Power, a spiritual Essence, Substance, or Law which comes to us from the within-ness we achieve. It is a Something that becomes tangible to us when our human thinking stops and when we no longer have opinions or desires—when we can sit, regardless of the form

86

of sin, disease, death, lack, or limitation that is appearing to us as person, place, thing, or condition, and inwardly listen, attune ourselves, be receptive, and wait until that emanation comes from within.

When that comes, you will find that something deeper and greater than yourself will flow out into visible expression. It, then, will do what we interpret as healing work, although actually what appears as healing work will be the dissolution of material sense. When there is no material sense, there is no personal sense of "I" to sin, to be sick, or to be poor. Only the little "I" can be rich or poor, only the human "I" can be sick or well, happy or unhappy; but when there is no longer any personal "I", what is left? God! God is left, God, the only *I*; God, the *I* that I am; God, manifesting Itself as the Son; God, the Father, appearing as God, the Son, in all of God's glory.

What hides that glory? What covers it up? Material sense—the veil of illusion. Material sense cannot be dissolved physically, nor can it be dissolved mentally: It can only be dissolved by bringing into conscious expression that inner Something which Paul called the Christ, and which Jesus called the Father within:

I can of mine own self do nothing . . .[1] the Father that dwelleth in me, he doeth the works.[2] . . . For it is God which worketh in you both to will and to do of his good pleasure.[3]

This is an inner feeling, an inner at-one-ment, an inner peace, and the moment you have this inner

[1] John 5:30.   [2] John 14:10.   [3] Philippians 2:13.

87

release, that is the sign of the Christ, or Emmanuel, God with us.

You have often heard people say, "Oh, trust God; believe in God; leave it to God." No Infinite Way student should ever make the mistake of indulging in such blind faith or wishful thinking unless he has experienced some assurance of God's presence. Such assurance comes in the stillness—in quietness and in confidence. "The still small voice" is heard when the outer ears and eyes are closed and the inner ear and inner eye are open.

Error Is Material Sense Appearing as Form

All sin, disease, lack, and limitation, and all wars are forms of material sense. *When material sense is destroyed, there is no substance out of which those forms can appear.* When this great truth is learned, there will come a time when we are no longer concerned with healings because most of our human errors fade away, and from then on, we take no thought about discord of any kind, but live merely to experience this realized Christ, letting the realized Christ live our lives for us and attract to us the persons, circumstances, and conditions necessary to our unfoldment.

We do not try to attract customers to our business or patients and students to our ministry: We achieve an inner realization of God's presence and let that unfold as It will. Then we find that it is literally true that all things are added unto us—by Grace, not by might or by power, not by our efforts, not by our thoughts. "For my thoughts are not your thoughts, neither are your ways my ways . . .[1] He uttered his

[1] Isaiah 55:8.

voice, the earth melted."[1] When God's thoughts touch us, the earth melts and with it every form of discord. What is left when the earth melts? God, Himself, Spirit—Spirit formed, Spirit manifest. Material sense is gone—melted, dissolved—*when He utters His voice.*

Let us remember our goal, whether we accomplish it this month or whether it take us a century. The goal is that we hear this Voice uttering Itself within us. When that Voice uttered Itself in Christ Jesus, all error dissolved before him; when that Voice uttered Itself in the disciples of Christ Jesus, all error melted before them; and when that Voice utters Itself in the consciousness of any individual, evil cannot stand before It, because evil is only a form of material sense. *The nature of all error is material sense appearing as form.*

The Dissolution of Material Sense Destroys Its Forms

There is no use in trying to get rid of the *form* of error. In other words, do not try to rid yourself of disease, lack, or limitation. These are only the decoys. They are the forms which error assumes, but error in all its forms is nothing but material sense, and material sense is dissolved only by spiritual consciousness. The Voice, the divine Presence, Emmanuel, God with us, Tao, Brahm—call It what you will, It is God in action. When God is active in your consciousness, material sense is dissolved; and when material sense is dissolved, the *forms* of material sense disappear.

Have you ever seen displays of huge pieces of ice

1 Psalm 46:6.

formed as birds, eagles, or rocks—pieces of ice carved into lifelike forms of fish or animals? What happens when the ice melts? The animals and fish disappear, and there is nothing left but a pool of water. All evil is nothing more nor less than a block of ice called material sense, and nothing will dissolve it except a realization of the presence of God. When you have a realization of God's presence, material sense is dissolved and with it all its forms: False appetite disappears; false desires disappear; lonesomeness disappears; homelessness disappears; lack and limitation, disputes between capital and labor, and even wars disappear. God-realization dissolves all forms as which material sense appears.

Never again can we hate as much as we did before; never again can we be as sensual or as sensuous as we were before, as greedy or avaricious. We cannot be as fearful or doubtful either, because all these are forms of material sense. As material sense is dissolved, fear, doubt, hate, jealousy, animosity, greed, and lust—all these disappear. But never try to get rid of the forms of error: Attain God-realization and let that dissolve the substance of the forms.

If you think of The Infinite Way as a method by which you will get God to do something for you or if you believe that you can turn to God for some form of good, you will miss the way. This teaching does not reveal a God who heals; it does not reveal a God who will send you supply; it does not reveal a God who will bring you companionship or happiness: It reveals God as Omnipresence and teaches you how to come into that realization of God and to let that realization live your life. Attaining a realization of God is the sole goal and the keynote of The Infinite Way.

In achieving a realization of God, you will quickly discover that you will never have to take thought for health or wealth or companionship or whatever else is needed to make your experience harmonious. Nothing is necessary to you but God-realization. Nothing will make for you a spiritually lived life, a spiritually endowed life, and a spiritually maintained and sustained life except the realization of God—the realization of God with you, the realization of that still small Voice uttering Itself and dissolving material sense.

Let us never be ensnared into believing that this means that God-realization will dissolve the material sense of all our friends, relatives, or neighbors. No, this realization dissolves the material sense through which we have been beholding our relatives, friends, and neighbors. The realization of God's presence dissolves material sense for us and in turn helps to do it for those who bring themselves consciously within range of our consciousness. Our nearest and dearest may be left in the very material sense that they seem to enjoy while a complete stranger may be attracted and come to us for the blessing that we have received through God-consciousness.

Jesus dissolved material sense insofar as he himself was concerned, and he dissolved it for those who would permit themselves to be shorn of their material sense, but certainly the record of the Master's career indicates that he did not succeed with those who insisted on clinging to material sense.

When others come to us in order that material

sense in them may be dissolved by virtue of their contact with us and because of whatever measure of light we have found, we then can become our brother's keeper, sharing the glory that we have found with those who desire it. Our concern is the attainment of that God-realization which is the destruction of material sense and which thereby removes its forms. And who can limit the scope of such realization?

Healing Without Mental Argument

Do not try to heal, supply, or employ anyone; do not try to secure companions for anyone or parking spaces or transportation: Try only, with every call, to attain an inner realization of God, and then let that do the work. It may do it in a far different way than you could ever outline. Certainly, It will do it in a far better way than you could ever plan. We do not know the ways of God, and certainly God knows nothing about our aimless flounderings and meanderings.

If you try to demonstrate *things*, you will not succeed. You can only hope to succeed in one thing —realizing God, realizing the Christ. If you succeed in that, the realized Christ will be the saviour unto any and every situation. When you stop being concerned about reducing fevers, dissolving lumps, knitting bones, getting employment, or bringing peace on earth—when you stop taking thought—and give your whole life's devotion to attaining the realization of the Christ, watch the miracles of Grace that follow. If necessary, water will flow from the rock; if necessary, the waters will divide. Nothing is impossible to God.

To heal without mental argument means to be able to sit quietly in that receptive state which we call meditation and wait patiently for the Voice to speak or for that feeling to come which brings with it the assurance that God is on the field. In order to lift yourself to a place above thoughts where there is only a deep stillness, it may be necessary to know the truth consciously, that is, to repeat it to yourself or to think it; but the student who has been on the spiritual path for some time and has made the contact often enough lives in it so completely that it is necessary only to close the eyes and almost instantly be at the center of his being.

It is not what you may know or what you may think or what you may read that does the healing work. It is an actual realization, an actual feeling within, of the presence and power of God immediately with us. Students must realize that they cannot expect too much from any spiritual treatment or work unless that treatment or work is accompanied by a realization of the Christ, by a feeling of the presence of God. Their treatment is not aimed at curing anything or anybody, but is solely for the purpose of lifting them into an atmosphere where the realization of spiritual harmony dawns, and then from within comes the assurance of God's allness, omnipotence, omnipresence, and omniscience.

When they have felt the presence of God, they have the right to expect manna to fall from the sky, if it has to appear in that way. They will see the lame walk, the deaf hear, the blind open their eyes, and even the dying rise to their feet. Is there anything impossible to God? No, God can set a table in the wilderness. Nothing is impossible to God, but we have to be sure that God is on the field, and our function is to achieve the realization of God, which in turn brings the demonstration of God.

FULFILLMENT

Through the daily practice of meditation, we learn to bring God into every experience. God, then, becomes the health of our body, the harmony of our relationships, and the activity of our day. "Except the Lord build the house, they labour in vain that build it: except the Lord keep the city, the watchman waketh but in vain."[1]

Most of us forget that there is a Presence within us which performs whatever is given us to do, a Presence which is our strength and our sure defense. Instead, we believe that we are responsible for accomplishing such tasks as are required of us, that we of ourselves perform the work each day, forgetting that "He performeth the thing that is appointed for me" to do.[2]

God made you in His own image and likeness and has provided everything necessary for your fulfillment. God has bestowed upon you the gift of His grace, and you are but an instrument of that Grace. Infinity is the measure of your being, and by the grace of God, you are God's witness to His infinite wisdom, abundance, and love. Never desire that any good *come* to you: Desire only that good be revealed *through* you; desire only that God's grace flow through you to all those who do not yet know the infinite nature of their own being; seek only to

[1] Psalm 127:1.   [2] Job 23:14.

be a fitting instrument through which God expresses, manifests, and reveals Itself to the world.

You have no demonstration to make: Your demonstration was made for you since before Abraham was, and that demonstration is your sonship with God, a relationship established in the beginning by God, Himself. Your only demonstration is the realization of this divine sonship—the realization that you are the heir of God and joint-heir with Christ to all the heavenly riches. You do not have to earn or deserve that inheritance: You need only acknowledge that it is already yours. Acknowledge the infinite nature of your own being; acknowledge the infinite nature of God's storehouse already established within you, and then, each day, turn within to the Divinity within you and let It flow in the acknowledgment of Omnipresence.

"Except the Lord build the house, they labour in vain that build it." Except you understand that God is the source of your supply, the very avenue of your supply of any and every good, supply cannot flow forth from you in its fullness. It is vain for you to rise up early or to sit up late trying to demonstrate supply, health, or companionship. Only acknowledge God to be the source and the grace of your health, the substance of your supply, and the cement of your relationships, and God will reveal Itself to you as fulfillment. Realize that the kingdom of God is within you. One instant's realization of that inner kingdom, which is already established within you, enables that kingdom with all of its riches to flow out from you into form.

You can draw upon the infinite Source within you

95

for everything necessary for your fulfillment. Turn within daily, hourly. Learn to look away from every condition and circumstance in the external realm and place your entire faith, hope, and reliance on the Infinite Invisible. God, Itself, is the answer to every problem. The supply of God's presence is the only supply you will ever need because you will find that in that Presence all things are included. "In thy presence is fulness of joy; at thy right hand there are pleasures for evermore."[1]

"The earth is the Lord's, and the fulness thereof . . .[2] Son, thou art ever with me, and all that I have is thine."[3] *I*, within you, is multiplying out of the unseen resources of Spirit—not drawing upon the visible resources of the earth, but drawing forth the infinite abundance of God from the invisible storehouse within your own being.

The moment you acknowledge that "the earth is the Lord's, and the fulness thereof," you give up any sense of possession of the things of the outer world. As you recognize the invisible nature of supply, supply then begins to express as tangible form. But whatever its form, it will pour forth as such an abundant blessing that there will not be room enough to receive it. The flow will begin the moment you acknowledge:

This is the house of the Lord, the house built by the Lord, His holy temple, and everything therein belongs to Him— my body, my relationships, my supply. The silver is the Lord's; the gold is the Lord's; the earth and all the fullness thereof belong to God—and yet all these riches are mine to use and enjoy by virtue of divine sonship.

[1] Psalm 16:11.   [2] Psalm 24:1.   [3] Luke 15:31.

In this realization, you will never again count what is in the visible world as the measure of your supply. Never again will you be concerned with how much or how little of the world's goods you may have, with whether there is economic prosperity or depression. None of that has anything to do with you, because you are Self-maintained and Self-sustained.

God Is Fulfilling Itself as Individual Being

Everything comes to you by the grace of God. As you begin to experience that Grace, you learn that the storehouse of all good is within your own being. God has given you His bounty and there is no limit to that bounty. It is only limited when you think that you have to go out into the world to earn it, that you have to be deserving of it, or that you have to go out into the world and achieve it by your own ingenuity. Turn from such limitation in the realization that God is infinite in being and expression, and that the infinity of God—the limitlessness of God—is pouring through you, pouring through you as fulfillment, God fulfilling Itself as your individual being.

God neither gives, nor does God withhold, and certainly, man who is but the instrument of God has no power to withhold. Therefore, you are never dependent upon the good will of any man. If you can relax and lose concern for yourself and for your welfare, you will find that God takes over, and God fulfills Itself by providing you with the necessary wisdom, activity, opportunity, and prosperity—not because of you, but in order that God, Itself, may be fulfilled on earth as It is in heaven. Do you not see that this earth is only the earth in proportion as we see it as a place other than heaven? Do you not see that there is no such thing as heaven *and* earth—that heaven and earth are one? Earth becomes heaven when you realize that God fulfills Itself as your individual experience.

The responsibility is on His shoulders. Do you not see how much less responsibility you have when you comprehend the nature of God as fulfillment? Your personal responsibility grows less and less as your recognition increases that God is fulfilling Its destiny on earth as your individual experience.

"Thou wilt keep him in perfect peace, whose mind is stayed on thee."[1] The important word to remember in that passage is the word "stayed". To keep the mind stayed on God is to obey Paul's injunction: "Pray without ceasing."[2] Give honor and glory unto God; acknowledge Him in all thy ways, and He will give thee peace, rest, comfort, and all the good things of life. To experience the life and peace of God, it is necessary to bring God into conscious remembrance and to dedicate every day to the service and the glory of God that everything we do may reflect glory unto God, that everything we think may be divinely wise, divinely loving, and divinely just.

Acknowledge God

We have come to this quiet hour only to keep the mind stayed on God and to contemplate God and the things of God, because God is the source of all

[1] Isaiah 26:3. [2] I Thessalonians 5:17.

that is. In God's presence is fullness of joy. Every blessing that is upon this earth is an emanation, or an expression, of God—the sun that warms us; the rain that feeds our plants, our vegetables, and flowers; the processes of nature that form the diamonds down under the surface of the earth, and the iron and the oil. All of these expressions of God-life are given to us for our use: The fertile earth to bring forth trees, fruits, vegetables, and flowers; the fish in the sea and elements that have not yet been extracted from the sea; the birds winging toward the sun. All of these are God's gift to man.

The stars, the tides, the moon—all fulfill functions of God and yet appear as blessings to man. Yes, even the sun, God hung up in the sky, millions of miles away from the earth, but just far enough away to give us the right amount of warmth and the right amount of coolness. Such law and order could not be accidental; it must be the activity of a divine Intelligence, an Intelligence which is love and wisdom. Yes, God's love is made evident in all things: Even before man appeared on earth, everything necessary for his development, for his growth, and for his welfare—for his fulfillment—was here.

Acknowledge God as the great Giver of the universe, the great Giver of Itself to the universe— God giving Its own intelligence, wisdom, direction, and strength to all that is. We are not something separate and apart from God.

God is the Father and God is the Son, and God has incarnated Itself as my very being—my intelligence, my life, my love, my Spirit, my strength. How close God is to me—closer than breathing, nearer than hands or feet!

99

I have no fears; I have no doubts. I do not have to reach out or up for God because God is both the Father and the Son; God is my very own being. I do not have to pray to God, nor do I have to ask favors of God or affirm some truth about God. I have only to acknowledge God, acknowledge that God is my being. Wherever I go, God goes with me— a Presence around me, beside me, and within me; wherever God is, that is where I am, ever-present. How glorious that is! Right where I am, God is, with all His bounty, with all His grace, His love, and His joy.

Filled with the realization of His power, I can do all things: "I can do all things through Christ which strengtheneth me.[1] *. . . I live; yet not I"*[2]*; it is really God living in me and through me. Thy Presence goes before me to prepare the way, to make smooth the rough places, to lead me beside the still waters where the noise and tumult of the world never penetrate.*

In God's presence, I can relax, rest, and let go of all the problems of the world—my world. God worketh hitherto, and I work. God works, God leads, God guides, God directs; and my function is to contemplate God, to contemplate these great truths of God, these great wisdoms and wonders of God.

Open the door for God to enter into your daily life by giving your firstfruits to God. "Bring ye all the tithes into the storehouse, that there may be meat in mine house, and prove me now herewith, saith the Lord of hosts, if I will not open you the windows of heaven, and pour you out a blessing, that there shall not be room enough to receive it."[3] Upon awakening in the morning, let your first thought be of God—a remembrance of God's loving kindness,

[1] Philippians 4:13.   [2] Galatians 2:20.   [3] Malachi 3:10.

God's wisdom and protection. Give praise and thanksgiving to God as you sit down to breakfast or to any other meal. As you undertake the work of each day, let your first thought be of God's infinite wisdom which maintains and sustains you in that work; and in recognition of that wisdom and power, give the firstfruits of your earnings to God. "Honour the Lord with thy substance, and with the firstfruits of all thine increase."[1] Let every activity and function of your life—business, social, civic—be performed in the acknowledgment of God as the source and the direction:

Father, this is Your day, the day which You have made. You made the sun to rise and You have given us its light and warmth; You have given us the cooling rains and the snows in their season. This is Your day, the day in which I will magnify Your name.

It is Your intelligence that I need today, Father—not my limited wisdom, but Your infinite wisdom. I need all the love with which You can fill me today. Let Your wisdom and Your love be expressed through me. Without You, Father, I am nothing—I can do nothing.

Use me this day, for as the heavens declare Your glory and the earth showeth forth Your handiwork, so must I show forth Your glory. Let Your will be made manifest in me, and let Your grace flow from me and through me to all those whom I meet upon life's highway. Grant me the assurance today that Your love is with me, that Your wisdom guides me and Your presence upholds me. In that assurance, I go forth with joy, knowing that God is fulfilling Itself as this day.

And so I resign myself to You, Father. I give myself to

[1] Proverbs 3:9.

You. I am Your son, forever held in Your love—safe in Your keeping. Be Thou ever with me.

ACROSS THE DESK

In February, a number of students came over to Hawaii for special study, and now in March more are here and more coming each month, so I shall remain at home at least until August.

Two reels of the Maui 1959 Advanced Work and four of the Halekou 1959 Special Group Work have been recorded so far this year and are ready for distribution. Soon there will be additional recordings available because, as students come to Halekou Place from far and near for instruction and meditation, this special work is being recorded so that those who are unable to be present for the work may participate in this experience through the recordings.

I am happy to announce that L. N. Fowler and Co., Ltd., of London, has *God the Substance of All Form* on the press. A reprint of the chapter, "A Circle of Christhood," from *The Art of Meditation*, has been published by *Triangle Magazine* of England in their British edition and in their foreign editions in the Dutch, German, French, Spanish, Italian, and Greek languages. *Truth for Business and Professional People* is now being translated into French by Unité Universelle in Paris.

Every day my mail brings to this desk accounts of the struggle students have to keep attention on God-realization when specific problems are acute. The temptation inevitably arises to attempt, first, to get rid of the pain, and after that has been accomplished, then, to settle down to seeking the kingdom of God; or first, to find that suitable position, home, or place of peace and quiet, and then give oneself to attaining the Christ.

Of course, this can never be successful because the pain will not yield, the position or home will not appear, nor will the peace and quiet come until spiritual realization is attained. One of my Unity friends says that what we are seeking is the secret of life itself. I think it will help everyone to realize that our whole effort must be directed to finding this secret. Do you not see how quieting it is to remember that when we have the secret of life itself, we have that which provides life eternal, harmonious, joyous, and abundant?

Please keep in mind that there is no human way of arriving at the goal of peace on earth, nor is there any human solution to the sins of the world or the inequalities so evident in human affairs. All these problems can be solved only by "seeking the secret of life itself." The truth-students and seekers after spiritual wisdom must first demonstrate that, by attaining God-realization, they are released from material sense, the source of all inharmony.

Would you like to witness the miracle of Grace? If you are among those of our students who do not yet "say grace" before meals, begin the practice before each meal of *silently* and *secretly* acknowledging God as That which sets the table—even in the wilderness—and acknowledge God as the bread, wine, water, and meat of life.

SPECIFIC TRUTH FOR TREATMENT

THE nature of specific treatment is a subject about which too many of our students know far too little, although it is probably one of the most important subjects included in the teaching of The Infinite Way, because everything which takes place in our experience has to take place in and through our own consciousness: We cannot live outside our own consciousness; we cannot even die outside our own consciousness. Everything that happens to us from birth to death and, for that matter, everything before birth and after death is an activity of our consciousness.

Therefore, no treatment that you can give will be any better than your knowledge of treatment, nor will it have any more power in it than your own consciousness of truth because *a treatment is your consciousness of truth.* Therefore, the success of a treatment will be in direct proportion to your consciousness of truth.

A successful treatment cannot be some kind of a fuzzy, vague, half-hearted statement, nor can it be in the realm of such generalities as, "God is all," or, "God is love." Whether you realize it or not, even if it is a treatment in which there are no words or thoughts, it has to be specific. Furthermore, a specific treatment without words or thoughts is only possible after you have gained such an awareness of the truth that you do not have to put it into words or thoughts: The words or thoughts have become realized consciousness.

In your highest spiritual realization, there is no need for words or thoughts. For example, if under ordinary circumstances you call upon me for help, I would not have to think a thought or declare a truth, but I would be a perfect vacuum. The healing would be accomplished because the consciousness of truth developed over a period of years of practice has given me the conviction that I am, and if I am, you are, and all that I am, you are—but I *know* that. I know that this is truth because of all the years of demonstration and because this truth has been proved over and over again and is now embodied in my consciousness.

If you should ask me, "How much is 12×12?" I would not have to think out the answer. But on the other hand, if you should ask a person who does not know that 12×12 is 144, he would have to engage in a process of thinking to arrive at the correct answer. The minute 2×2 is 5 hits up against my consciousness, I do not have to think consciously about the problem because I am not fooled by 5 when I know that the answer is 4. But what about children in the primary grades in school who have not yet learned that 2×2 equals 4? They will have to develop a consciousness of this mathematical fact through many different concrete experiences: two apples and two apples, two books and two books, two pennies and two pennies, developing through each experience an awareness that 2×2 or $2 + 2$ of anything is 4. They may have to repeat this learning process many, many times before they are able to respond automatically with 4.

Every Problem Has a Specific Answer

So it is when you are asked for spiritual help. Let us assume that the call is a request for help with no further explanation forthcoming. You do not know whether it is physical, mental, moral, or financial. In response to that call, all you can do is to turn within, and if you have learned to take God as the first word of any treatment—which you must learn to do—you will dwell on some of the principles of spiritual healing:

God—God is the substance of all form; God is the source of all activity, God—the Essence and Substance. All health, all action, all harmony, and all supply are in Cause, not effect. Then all harmony, peace, jurisdiction, and good are in God, the Cause.

That may be enough for you to know, and with that you are satisfied: You have declared your "4." Now you are ready for that second part of the treatment in which you wait for the confirmation to come from within.

Probably in most cases, however, when someone asks for help, he will explain the nature of his problem. It may be a physical disease, which he may even mention by name, such as one of the contagious diseases so prevalent in winter—colds, "flu," or the grippe. Again you begin with God, and quickly or slowly, you come to realize that, because God is infinite and omnipresent, every quality and activity emanates from Him, and if there were such a thing as infection or contagion in the world, then it would have to come from God. Thus you would not be denying infection. In fact, you might even acknowledge that there is infection, but what could emanate from God as infection or contagion other than the qualities of God? Then all the children of God must, and can, only be infected with the qualities of God, and only these qualities could be contagious because all this activity is taking place in the spiritual realm, in the realm of good, in the realm of incorporeality.

With such an understanding of the nature of infection and contagion, fear would be dissolved. That word "incorporeality" might come to you, and with it the realization that, if infection and contagion are incorporeal, they do not have to be feared. Then would come a sense of satisfaction, a settling back, that deep breath, or "click"—that sense of release.

Another call comes that somebody has had a stroke or an accident, is paralyzed, and therefore cannot walk properly or may not be able to move his arms. Quickly it comes, and after you have had a little experience, instantly:

The body cannot move; of itself, it is inert. An arm has no power to move itself: I move the arm; I have to do that. An arm left to itself will remain where it is indefinitely, because if it is to move, there has to be an I to move it. And what is that I but God? That I is the source, substance, and activity of body, the only law governing the body.

Now once again you are at peace. You have achieved a quietness and calm; that "click," or deep breath, comes, and you are free.

The next call may be from somebody who is having financial difficulty. Why or in what way makes no difference. It could be because of unemployment; it could be that the person's money is tied up in property; it could be any kind of trouble of an economic nature. Whatever the nature, if you are in a high enough state of consciousness, almost instantly will come the realization:

"The earth is the Lord's, and the fulness thereof."[1] *All the abundance which fills the earth to overflowing is the Father's, but has He not promised, "Son . . . all that I have is thine"*[2]*? Was that addressed to one son only? No, God is not a respecter of persons; God does not have favorites! That promise was given to all the children of God. It is a universal truth in which I can rest.*

Again you go into the silence, achieve your peace, and then you have come to the end of that treatment.

On another occasion, you may receive word that a devastating hurricane is on the way. Again you will begin your treatment with the word God:

God is infinite. Then there can be no place where God is and at the same time a hurricane operating—unless it is a very spiritual hurricane, which in that case would be a blessing. If God is infinite, there cannot be a place where the infinite goodness of God is not in expression. Therefore, nothing destructive can be present.

That is all. Then comes that period of silence which brings your awareness of the Presence. Notice that again this is specific treatment.

You may receive a thousand different answers to the foregoing problems, but you may be sure that there will always be some specific answer to every

[1] Psalm 24:1.   [2] Luke 15:31.

problem. For example, if your problem is 8×8, your answer will not be 4, nor will it be 144, but 64. In every case of healing, effectively handled, there is always a specific answer to a specific problem.

It is only after you have gone through this process thousands of times that you finally arrive at a place where it is no longer necessary to do that. It has become so thoroughly established in you that you do not have to sit down and consciously think truth. You know it; it is established; it is what you already are, what constitutes your being.

Perhaps the illustration of the difference between a skilled typist and one of the hunt-and-peck variety, such as I am, will clarify this point. If I should sit down to a typewriter, I would have to look at every key and watch carefully to see that my fingers hit the right keys. An expert typist does not have to proceed so laboriously, because he is able to strike the right keys without looking at them and without even thinking about them. The process has become automatic. It is the same with playing the piano. What kind of a pianist would have to watch the keyboard? My kind! But no pianist of any ability would be so hampered in his execution of a composition because the fingers of a competent pianist automatically strike the right notes.

And so it is in the practice of spiritual healing. After you have dealt with enough claims of colds, "flu," grippe, pneumonia, or consumption, you know the solution so thoroughly that when any one of these problems is presented to you, your only response is a smile.

Every day, you encounter people who habitually

voice negative ideas and fears about the world. How often have you heard somebody say, "Oh, these are very bad times! You'll see, things are going to get worse and worse!" Did hearing such remarks amuse you when you remembered how many millionaires have been made during "bad times"? On the other hand, there is the person who loudly shouts, "These are unusually good times—boom times," and then you wonder if this person with his optimistic outlook is aware of the families down the street who are struggling to make ends meet. The truth of the matter is that no one is a victim of the times: The times are in His hands. There are not good times or bad times: There are only God-times for those who practice the presence of God; and for those who live in a world without God, there are only the godless times of chance and change.

Specific Truth Is Universally True

In spiritual healing, the treatment is never given to a Mrs. Jones, a Mr. Smith, or a Miss Brown. The treatment is never given to an old man, a middle-aged woman, a young adult, an adolescent, or an infant. Such a treatment has no place in spiritual healing, because 2×2 is 4 whether it refers to apples, peaches, plums, pineapples, dollars, doughnuts, millions, or billions. In other words, whatever truth you know is a universal truth and is not just the truth about you or me.

Unfortunately, too often religion has taught that we can go to God asking Him for something for you or for me which will be given to us to the exclusion of everyone else in the world. The Infinite Way emphasizes—and this teaching is probably unique to The Infinite Way—that God could not any more do that than He could make 2 × 2 equal 4 when applied to peaches, but not when applied to plums. When 2 × 2 is 4, it is 4, universally and impersonally, for a sinner as well as for a saint.

When you present a problem to me, whatever the truth is that I know, it is not merely the truth about you: It is the truth, period. It is universal. Therefore, I do not have to direct the truth to you just because you have asked for help. If the truth I know is a universal truth, it has to be the truth about you. That is why it is not necessary to know the name of the patient. In fact, you do not even have to be told whether it is a cat or a dog or a human being, because any truth that you know is truth, period.

It is probably true, however, that the less experience you have had with healing work, the more you should know about the claim, because until a healing consciousness has been established the more specific you would have to be in your treatment. I remember a call that came to me many years ago that had to do with an infant suffering from one of the diseases of early childhood. The very first thought that flashed into my mind was: "There are no infants. God has never been and can never be an infant, and God is the only being there is. God is the only life there is, the only mind, the only Soul, the only Spirit." That ended the treatment. But at that point of my development, it was helpful to know that the patient was an infant because it focused my attention on knowing the truth about infants. And what is the truth about infants? There are no infants in "My kingdom."

Do you see also that in some cases it might be helpful for you to know that a disease is peculiar to a man or a woman because you then might realize:

There is only God-being, and that God-being is both male and female in quality. There is no corporeality in God; and therefore, the male and female of God's creating are not corporeal male and female, but male and female in quality of being.

All this is necessary, however, only in the early stages of your healing ministry. After you have worked with ten thousand cases, it would make no difference to you who or what your patient is, male or female, infant or aged, animal or plant, because instinctively you would realize that these cases are coming to you from "this world," where such distinctions exist. *Your treatments, however, are never on the level of "this world."*

Two of the most powerful teachings in The Infinite Way are found in the scriptural passages, "My kingdom is not of this world"[1] and, "Man shall not live by bread alone."[2] The minute a problem is presented to you, and you can realize, "My kingdom is not of this world," that is the end of the problem so far as you are concerned. You are not patching up this universe; you are not healing physical bodies. You are not dealing with problems of middle age or old age or adolescence. All that is eliminated the minute you realize, "My kingdom [the spiritual kingdom] is not of this world." Then you do not have to come down to any specific treatments, and

[1] John 18:36.   [2] Matthew 4:4.

yet even in meeting problems in this way you are doing specific work because you are meeting the claims of "this world."

In other words, never feel that you are so high spiritually that you do not think it necessary to give specific help, even if that specific help is only addressed to a "this world." I do not honestly believe, however, that our younger students can stand on that high a plane because to them "this world" is too real. Even if intellectually they claim it is not, they are only lying to themselves. They are unaware of this, but the fact of the matter is that many people unwittingly lie to themselves, and often the very ones who most vehemently disclaim this are the worst offenders.

Furthermore, no treatment will be effective if it contains anything that insults your intelligence. It should satisfy you at your level of consciousness. Therefore, be as specific as you find it necessary to be in your treatment, but never stop your healing work with the treatment. Always remember to take that second step of becoming still and waiting for the seal to be placed on the treatment, for that "click," that inner release, because that is the major part of the treatment.

Healing and Teaching Go Hand in Hand

When you undertake a healing ministry—and I do not necessarily mean setting yourself up in an office as a practitioner, but just in your homes as people come to you for help—you will be asked questions on any and every subject that concern everyday living, and you should be able to give satisfactory answers to every one of these questions.

For example, there is not a week of the year that someone does not ask me whether or not he should leave his church or join a church. Such questions should not be answered categorically or with a vague generalization such as "God is love." There must be a specific answer, and such an answer might well be, "Fulfill yourself at your present level. If you feel the need for a church, by all means attend or belong to one." On the other hand, to the question of leaving the church, an appropriate answer might be, "No, not until it is definitely established in you that you should take this step. When that is clear to you, you will not even ask the question—you will go ahead and act. So long as you are asking the question, you are not ready to withdraw your membership." When you give answers such as these to this type of question, you have not left your student floundering, but have given him something to think about.

Somebody may want to know if he should or should not eat meat. For you to tell him that God is truth will not help him very much, but you might remind him that he can live only at the level of his own consciousness. If he is at a point where he enjoys meat or seems to require it, he should continue eating it. When it is no longer needed in his experience, the habit of eating meat will drop away, and he will not have to ask the question.

There are hundreds of questions that will be thrown at you, each one requiring a definite answer: What do you believe about the immaculate conception? What is your teaching in regard to the

Resurrection? What do you know about the Ascension? What is your concept of immortality? What do you know about the nature of God? What is your understanding of the nature of prayer? If you do not have the understanding and background requisite to enable you to be specific in answering these questions, you not only cannot teach the principles of The Infinite Way, but you cannot even give a good treatment, because a treatment is a concrete knowing of the truth: "Ye shall know the truth, and the truth shall make you free."[1] How are you going to "know the truth" if you do not know it? Knowing the truth involves much more than merely mouthing such phrases as "God is love" or "God is truth."

Attaining the God-Is-All State of Consciousness

Some schools of metaphysics would reject this teaching of specific treatment because they would claim that, inasmuch as God is all, specific treatment is unnecessary. I do not deny that God is all, but I challenge anyone to prove that the allness of God is going to do very much for a person until he knows the truth—and the truth he has to know must be a specific truth.

For example, a specific truth would be a recognition that you do not live because your heart is beating, but that your heart is beating because you are living. You do not live by the organs and functions of your body, but the truth entertained in your consciousness acts upon them, and they operate harmoniously because of the *I* of your being. *I*

[1] John 8:32.

govern the heart, the liver, and the lungs—every organ of the body. These organs function because of *I*. Would it not be a hopeless way of life to believe that *I* live because of them? That would mean that when something happens to them, then *I* would cease to exist, but *I* can never cease to exist because *I* am life eternal.

So it is that the truth in your consciousness becomes a law unto your body, unto your business, and unto everything in your experience. That does not mean, however, that every time you receive a call some specific statement of truth has to rise up out of consciousness because gradually truth becomes so ingrained in your consciousness that *it is you*. When that day comes, your only response is a knowing smile, and that will be the end of the problem. But it is the end of the problem only because back of that smile, well established in your consciousness, is a knowledge of truth.

The great mystical poet, William Blake, wrote that you do not see with your eyes, but through your eyes.

There is an I *that functions through the body, but the body is not* I. *The body is an instrument given to me, and* I *have dominion over it. The body cannot walk;* I *walk. Strength is not in the muscles: Strength is in the Spirit, and It uses the muscles.*

That is knowing the truth. For every claim relating to the body and every suggestion of malfunctioning of the organs or bodily activity, there is a truth; for every business problem, in one form or another, there is a truth; for every appearance of untoward weather or climate, there is a truth—

and these specific truths must always be known.

It is true, in the final analysis, that all your knowing can be reduced to the simple statement, "God is all"; but by the time you have known specific truths for ten thousand or more cases, you will then be convinced that these truths which have taken the form of words or statements are true, and that God really is all, and then you will have reached the God-is-all state of consciousness. You will know what the statement, "God is all," means, and it will no longer be merely a cliché. When the words, "God is all," come to you, with them will come the awareness that God functions your body, God activates your business, God governs your home, and God appears as the substance of your supply. God is the essence, the substance, the activity, the law, and the cause of all form. Do you not see, therefore, that the words, "God is all," are meaningless until you have some understanding of all that God is?

Let Truth Be Revealed from Within

Let it be clearly understood that the wisdom of man is not sufficient to give anyone the specific truths adequate to meet a problem. When you are confronted with specific problems, whether your own or somebody else's, you cannot rush around looking for a memorandum of some recording you have heard or some passage in a book you have read to remind you what truths you are supposed to know, because, even if you found them instantly, they would not be too helpful.

When you are confronted with a problem of diseased organs or abnormal functioning of the body, and if at that moment you do not have firmly fixed in your being the truth that the *I* governs the organs and functions of the body and that the organs and functions of the body do not govern you, do not try to remember some truth, but immediately turn to the Father within and ask for the truth, and let that truth come to you from within.

The Infinite Way is not a method of memorizing and repeating truths which have been revealed to me. It is not the memorization of formulas. It is not a way of trying to teach you what truths to know, but rather how to discover truth so that you can learn this truth the same way in which I learned it.

All truth is given to us from God, and if you want to know the truth about anything—the specific truth—you do not have to go to a book to find it. Turn to the Father within. If you find that your plants are drooping and not doing well, do not run to a book to see what truth you should know. Turn within, and if you are patient, a truth will come to you, and soon your flowers will look up at you and begin to smile. We are not trying to build a spiritual consciousness based on memory, on knowledge, or on an exhaustive compilation of formulas, affirmations, and denials.

The reason for the emphasis on meditation in The Infinite Way is to teach you where and how to go to get any specific truth you need for any specific problem. You may be called upon this very night for some problem about which no one has ever even heard. In that case, obviously, it would be futile to look in any book for a solution because it could not be found there. You must learn to turn quickly—

instantaneously—within. Strangely enough by doing that, you may be led to open the Bible or some other book at just the right place. That has happened many, many times.

It was in just that way that the book, *Spiritual Interpretation of Scripture*[1], came into being. Students came to me and wanted to know something about the Bible, and because I did not know enough out of my human knowledge to teach them, each week before the lesson I turned within and asked, "Father, what lesson do You want the students to have?" In that state of receptivity, I found some story every time I opened the Bible, and the interpretation of that story was then revealed to me. For sixty weeks that continued with a new lesson unfolding to me every week—one that I had never known before. Every class since that time has unfolded in that same way with no foreknowledge of what was going to come through.

There is a specific truth for every problem, and the abiding place of that truth is in your consciousness. Your consciousness is the place where every bit of truth is found because *I am* the truth. *I*—the *I* of you and the *I* of me—embody the truth, all of it, not a little of it, but all of it. As students, you have to learn to go within and receive it from within.

You do not know when you seek within whether you are going to be able to go deep enough to find the "pearl of great price" or just cultured pearls. It often happens that at the most unexpected moments when you do not dream that anything

[1] By the author (San Gabriel, Calif.: Willing Publishing Co., 1947).

worthwhile is coming through, that is the very time when the real "pearls" reveal themselves. It is usually when we are called upon for help that we are given the gems that constitute the meat, wine, and water for the rest of our lives.

"The kingdom of God is within you."[1] There is nothing for which you could seek that you cannot find within yourself. When you learn to receive the answers, you will find that you are given a truth, a specific truth with which to meet every problem because there is a specific truth about every problem which will be revealed through turning wholeheartedly to God and in meditation seeking Him alone.

The question often arises as to whether or not God knows anything about our problems. Probably not, but when you go within asking, "What or where is the bread of this day?" the answer may come, "*I* am the bread, the wine, and the water." Or if you should ask what the truth is about a particular situation, you might hear the words, "*I* am the truth." The problem of the organs and functions of the body may be uppermost in your mind, and then truth may reveal itself in this way, "*I* govern the organs and functions of the body. Life governs the organs and functions of the body: Organs and functions do not govern life."

People with problems of paralysis, of muscles that will not move, may come to you, and as you go within, the answer again comes back, "*I* am the life of the body. *I* am the activity of the body. Spirit governs Its formations"; or some truth comes that

[1] Luke 17:21.

makes you realize that the body is not self-acting, that in and of itself it cannot move either for good or evil.

My conscious oneness with God constitutes my oneness with all spiritual creation, with everything that is necessary for my unfoldment. How did I learn that? That was imparted from within, but would it have been imparted to me from within if I had not learned to meditate? It is our meditations that bring forth whatever it is that we need to know at any moment.

If I should give you the truth for a specific problem—even a whole list of truths—it would be of no value to you because for you it would be merely a mentally perceived, and not a spiritually discerned, truth. It is only the spiritually discerned truth that meets your need. For example, not one of the words in this *Letter* is power: It is the word of God that is quick and powerful. Therefore, go within to the kingdom of God and let the still small voice utter Itself, and then when He utters His voice, the earth melts.

"He uttered his voice, the earth melted." If we become so proficient in the practice of the Presence that we can sit quietly with our attention focused on the Within, the still small voice will thunder, and the whole earth of evil will melt and fade out of our experience. It may come as an actual voice; it may come as a vision; but neither is necessary: Only one thing is necessary and that is to wait until there is a stirring or a feeling which is our assurance that God has uttered His voice.[1]

[1] By the author, *Practicing the Presence* (New York: Harper & Brothers, 1958). Pp. 109-10.

Contrary to the usual belief, when we go to God for something, we come away empty handed. That is a startling statement and one which, on first reading, may seem almost sacrilegious, but think back over your own life and note to what extent this is true.

In the early stages of our spiritual journey, we seek God in order that we may find peace, safety, health, and prosperity—and, in a measure, our circumstances and affairs do improve. As we continue on the spiritual path, we feel that even with better health, greater security, and more peace there is still something lacking. Meditation has opened the way in us to receive impartations from God—to hear the still small voice—and now it dawns in consciousness that we are to take the higher step of seeking God not for any benefits, but only for the joy of spiritual communion.

Watch the results when you seek God that you may serve Him, that you may show forth His glory, that you may come to know Him aright and to understand His ways and His kingdom. Watch the results when you relinquish the desire to get, to get anything—even from God.

As we turn now to the Bible and other writings, we find ourselves reading more for inspiration, for joy, and for light, rather than thinking of the results to be derived from such reading. It is then that "the added things" begin to flood our experience. "My kingdom is not of this world."[1] To

[1] John 18:36.

experience more of the good things of "this world," such as physical and mental wholeness and financial independence—even this does not constitute the kingdom of God, the spiritual realm of life. True, these are found when spiritual awareness is attained, but they are not the goal, nor can they be spiritually attained while they are being sought.

"My peace I give unto you: not as the world giveth."[1] In the following scriptural passages, note the similarity of ideas: "My kingdom is not of this world"; "My peace I give unto you: not as the world giveth"; and, "Seek not ye what ye shall eat, or what ye shall drink . . . but rather seek ye the kingdom of God."[2] Do you not see what the Master is trying to reveal to us? Do you begin to see what The Infinite Way is revealing to us when it teaches that we are not to seek more or better humanhood, but to meditate on God and the things of God until God-realization is experienced in our lives?

May I tell you that I have found this an exceedingly difficult task? In spite of my experience on the spiritual path and my intention always to seek God and God alone, unconsciously my aim was to be free of pain and disease and lack, to be full of health and harmony and abundance. It was so easy to declare and to think and even to believe that I was truly seeking the spiritual kingdom for myself and for those who came to me. Only intense prayer and an inner hunger and thirst compelled me to begin over again after every failure, until my desires could be purified.

Who in the world can truthfully say that he has

[1] John 14:27. [2] Luke 12:29, 31.

no concern for the harmonies and satisfactions of this world? Therefore, do not be too concerned if secretly you want better health, greater peace, or more supply, but admit it and then turn within for a purification of your desires and for greater devotion to the effort of attaining God's grace rather than more and better humanhood.

The way is not easy, but the attainment is so wonderful, so all satisfying, so joyous! I do not know how to picture spiritual freedom and harmony so that you can understand it intellectually, but I can reveal it to you and bring it into your experience in proportion to your faithfulness in holding to this goal. In our writings are found the steps leading to spiritual attainment, and all those on this Way can always be assured of my wholehearted help and co-operation.

It is early April, and every week more students come from far places to study with me. This work with students is recorded on the Halekou 1959 Special Group Work tapes, the Hawaiian Village tapes, and the Maui 1959 Advanced Work recordings.

SPIRITUAL FREEDOM

In the human scene, most people are primarily concerned with themselves, and after themselves, with their family, and after their family with their business or profession; but as they rise in spiritual consciousness, the problems of their community and those of their nation become important to them, and the higher they rise spiritually, the more keenly are they aware of world problems. It is doubtful if anyone can attain a very high level of spiritual consciousness without being made more aware of the world's problems than before he attained such spiritual consciousness.

Why must that necessarily be true? The answer can be found in the one word "freedom." Above all others, the spiritually illumined person understands the real meaning of freedom, and because he himself has experienced it, he longs to share that same freedom with the whole world. He has discovered that actually the only problem facing the world is a lack of freedom. The human race is not and never has been free. It is enslaved—physically, politically, and economically—first of all, by itself, within itself, and within its own body. Moreover, it is chained by the physical habits and by the political and economic theories and beliefs of generations. For example, witness the extent to which the entire race is in slavery to money. It is only the mystic who is free of the limiting belief that dollar bills, pounds sterling, or some other form of currency controls one's destiny.

The greater the heights of spiritual consciousness you reach, the more keenly will you become aware of the many, many forms of slavery which are binding men and women to a life of dissatisfaction and frustration, and simultaneously the stronger will become the urge within you to see them set free. That is why some people in the earliest stages of their spiritual growth become zealots with the drive of a Paul. They want to go out into the world and free all men, and like Paul, they often end up with broken bodies and minds because the world resists anything or anybody that attempts to bring some measure of freedom to it. The world usually bestows its honors and greatest wealth upon those who would enslave it, but ironically resists those who would set it free.

The further you go and the higher you progress in spiritual unfoldment, the more clearly will the picture of how men are mentally and physically enslaved stretch out before you as a vast panorama of tragedy; but, at the same time, because the remedy is also known to you, there is born in you the desire to help them achieve and maintain their freedom. Ultimately, wisdom will reveal ways in which to awaken men and women from their lethargy and inertia and arouse them to their responsibilities as citizens, thereby giving them at least some measure of freedom.

The way is straight and narrow and few there be who find it, and even many of those few who do find it, lose it. Your individual freedom—and by freedom I do not mean a freedom *from* anything, but *a freedom in Grace*—will come to you in proportion as you have a developed consciousness of truth which enables you to face any specific error and not fight it, but rather turn from it in the realization that the healing, redeeming, and freeing agency is the Christ realized, or God realized.

In striving to reach the goal of freedom, you will discover that the most difficult moment of all for you will come when you attempt to resolve your own problems of health or supply, or those of your family, community, or nation into their nothingness and find that instead of succeeding you are battling the very problems which intellectually you have recognized as nothingness. The fact is that in order to resolve these problems into the nothingness which they are, it is necessary to come to a place where you know that the battle is not yours, and that therefore you need no longer resist them. It is the inability to refrain from handling your problem as an "it" that presents the real difficulty.

When you sit down with a problem of any nature, it will be helpful if your first thought is of some one of the many biblical promises: "Where the Spirit of the Lord is, there is liberty,"[1] or, "In thy presence is fulness of joy."[2] That will instantly free you from any attempt to do battle with the problem because

[1] II Corinthians 3:17.   [2] Psalm 16:11.

it will immediately remind you that the object of your work is not the overcoming of a problem, but the attaining of God-consciousness.

Mental science teachings, psychology, and psychiatry differ from this approach in that they work on specific problems from the human standpoint, their objective being the changing of evil human conditions into good human conditions. The Infinite Way operates on an entirely different level of consciousness, in which we do not battle or overcome problems, nor attempt to supplant human evil with human good, but stand on the Master's revelation that "My kingdom is not of this world."[1]

The Infinite Way is founded on the revelation of this spiritual kingdom, a God-governed universe in which man does not live by physical might or mental power, but by *My Spirit*. He lives by the word of God, which is quick and sharp and powerful—not by the thoughts of man. The Infinite Way is based, not on mind-power, but on God-power, a power which is the very Soul of man, but which uses the mind as an instrument. When you battle a problem, you are fighting it with your mind; and therefore, you are making of your mind a power, instead of using it as an instrument.

If you allow your mind to be the instrument of your Soul, then when a problem confronts you, instead of battling or working against it, you will remember, first of all, that where the Spirit of the Lord is, there is freedom. In that assurance, you are able to drop the problem, thereby finding yourself receptive and responsive to the word of God. Your

[1] John 18:36.

mind, then, becomes an instrument through which you can hear the still small voice—or at least listen for it—and your attitude is one of receptivity, a recognition that the only problem you now have is to achieve a sense of God's presence.

You can bring to your thought any of the specific truths that you know, always reminding yourself that you are not attempting to heal or to enrich anybody, nor to solve their human problems, but to receive God's grace. You are sitting in meditation only to let God speak, for when He utters His voice, the earth melts. Therefore—and this is difficult—stop struggling against the problem; stop using physical might; stop using mental might; and learn to relax.

This is somewhat like becoming a vacuum, except that inwardly you are more awake and alert than ever before. In that stillness and quietness, that absence of everything that you have acknowledged as power, the Christ can come to you. Sometimes It comes very gently and peacefully, and sometimes It thunders, startling you. But when It speaks, the problems—personal, community, national, or international—are resolved; and physical, mental, moral, or financial freedom is attained—not by might, not by power, but by the grace of God.

The attainment to be sought is spiritual Grace. The way of that attainment is non-resistance within, that is, no mental resistance. Realize that where the Spirit of the Lord is, there is freedom; in His presence is fullness of life; His grace is your sufficiency. Such realization enables you to release yourself from the struggle; it frees your mind from its merry-go-round, even if it is but for two or three seconds, so that you can devote yourself to attaining the realization of God's presence, the Spirit of the Lord; and when It comes upon you, flooding you with that inner grace or sense of release, you will find that in some perfectly normal, natural way, the outer problem is solved.

The way to the solution of a problem or the solution itself takes place when your thought is not fastened upon it. The solution of the problem does not always unfold in the same way: Sometimes the problem dissolves without leaving a trace of it, and you are not aware of when it happens or why or how; at other times, you are given a specific answer as to when and what must or must not be done.

The grace of God is brought into expression when your human selfhood has been silenced. Then you are never concerned with a problem of any personal nature: You are concerned with but one problem, and that is that the world is living in a sense of separation from God, and because God is not functioning in its experience, it is in chains of slavery. Your only function is to be an instrument through which the voice of God can speak, as it did through Moses on Mount Sinai.

God Speaks Through Individual Consciousness

In Moses we have the figure of a man, humbly listening, searching, and seeking until in that humility, the Voice thundered through him. Although the Hebrews had been in slavery for generations, the moment the voice of God thundered in the consciousness of Moses, steps leading to their

130

ultimate freedom were set in motion—but never forget that that freedom began with the Voice thundering in the consciousness of *one individual.*

Centuries later, the Hebrews were again reduced to slavery by the Caesars, and in their desperation they prayed and dreamed of a Messiah who would come and set them free, a Messiah who would become their king and achieve a military victory in a war against the Caesars. But no such Messiah came. How could he? There is no such Messiah. When the Messiah comes, It reveals a whole new concept of power, a power which is not physical or mental: "Be still . . ."[1] in quietness and in confidence shall be your strength . . ."[2] Ye shall know the truth, and the truth shall make you free"[3]—not physical might or mental might will free you, but *the truth.* "Resist not evil."[4] Put up your sword, for those that live by the sword shall die by the sword, whether that sword be a physical sword or a mental sword. Put up your arguments, cease your fighting, stop your battling, so that the Spirit of the Lord God may be upon you. Then are you ordained to heal the sick, and the miracles of the Christ take place.

The presence and power of God cannot come through in a figure on a cloud. The presence and power of God come to earth through consciousness—through individual consciousness. Always there is a Moses, an Elijah or Isaiah, a Jesus or John, because the activity of God cannot be separated from individual consciousness. It is useless to wait for God to come to the collective consciousness of the world

[1] Psalm 46:10. [2] Isaiah 30:15.
[3] John 8:32. [4] Matthew 5:39.

131

or to wait for the power of the Christ to descend upon the world. It does not come in that way. It never comes separate and apart from consciousness: *It always comes through individual consciousness.* If It came to every person reading this *Letter*, and even if they all could be gathered in one room, It would still have to come to each one individually.

I have witnessed over and over again that the Christ comes to one, three, five, or six. During one class, the Christ became so evident that, out of a room of 400 people, 200 witnessed the experience, and miracles of healing took place. The other 200 were completely unaware of anything of an unusual nature transpiring. They never even knew that anything had taken place, and of course did not experience any healing, but only wondered why I had stopped talking.

The great miracles of life that take place through the activity of God come through some one individual. "I, if I be lifted up . . . will draw all men unto me."[1] God reveals Itself as consciousness, but that consciousness always appears to us as a man or a woman. In almost every generation, there have been one, two, three, or four mystics through whom miracles have been wrought. There was a Lao-tze, a Gautama, a Jesus, a John; there was a Bodhi-Dharma who carried the greatest message of Buddhism that the world has ever known from India to China and Japan; there was a Nanak in India who had one of the greatest religious teachings in the history of the world; and there were the Hebrew mystics who have given us some of the purest truths

[1] John 12:32.

that have ever been revealed. In every case, however, the teachings which were to free those who were willing to accept freedom came through, or as, an individual. Then the light of that one individual spread to twelve, to seventy, to two hundred, or to a thousand; and for one, two, or three generations afterwards, there was great spiritual light in the world.

It is true that history records that the light has always faded. It has always gone out; another civilization has been lost; and a period of darkness has ensued. That is probably why it has been revealed that "I will overturn, overturn, overturn . . . until he come whose right it is."[1] Until that spiritual consciousness becomes universal consciousness, there will be such overturnings, but in the periods of darkness a mystic here and there will appear to light the way. The work of these mystics will thrive for two, three, or four hundred years, and then be lost again; and this cycle will continue until, in some way not yet apparent to the world, the light will come on a more universal scale.

Eternal Vigilance Is the Price of Freedom

Because the world cries out for freedom, do not be misled into believing that it wants freedom. Search the annals of history. Can you find any nation which has achieved freedom that has been able to keep it? Always the people who have been given freedom in larger or lesser measure have eventually lost it because the drive within them for freedom has not been strong enough to keep them awake or sufficiently alert to protect it—not deep enough to make

[1] Ezekiel 21:27.

them willing to sacrifice for it. Just as you who are on the spiritual path are discovering that you cannot spiritually attain your health, your economic freedom, or your moral freedom by any quick or devious method, so you will ultimately learn that no nation can maintain physical health, moral fiber, financial solvency, or political stability by self-indulgence.

For us, the great realization is that there is a Kingdom. There is a spiritual Kingdom, a state of consciousness which is completely God-governed. Our lives are dedicated to the establishment of that Kingdom, in reality, dedicated to the development of it within our own being. "In my Father's house are many mansions"[1]—in that spiritual Kingdom are many and varied mansions, all of them harmonious, joyous, and free, translating themselves into human modes of life, a life not lived on a mountain top somewhere, separate and apart from the world, but lived right in this world, and usually lived in such a way as to make this human world a better place, first for you individually, and secondly for others who are led to you, and then on and on, on an ever widening basis.

The Wider Activity of The Infinite Way

The vast majority of those who come to The Infinite Way come for the solution of their individual problems, but if they go far enough in this work, they become a part of the few who are engaged in the wider activity of dealing with world problems. Never should we forget that we are engaged in an

[1] John 14:2.

activity that concerns greater problems than our individual health or supply, and that wider aspect is the next phase of the work of The Infinite Way.

As has been pointed out, whatever light has been given to the world has come through individual consciousness; but by reviewing the religious experience of the world, you will observe that, in spite of all the light that has come to us through the illumined souls down through the ages, the world is still in spiritual darkness. From that, it can be deduced that no amount of light coming from any one individual is sufficient to save the world, regardless of how bright it may be.

The light must come through a greater number of individuals, more and more of them at one time, until, ultimately, it permeates all individual consciousness and becomes collective consciousness. We have passed the day when any single individual, regardless of how illumined he may be, or may become, can be looked upon as anything more than a guide, pointing the way to what every individual may and must attain. Your goal, and mine, is the attainment of the greatest light of which we are capable, and then the acceptance of the responsibility for teaching it and making it available to others, so that in their turn they may be inspired to seek or become that same light. In no other way will spiritual freedom come to the world.

It will not come through one revelator, nor will it come through six revelators. True, the secret may come through one person, as it has a dozen times, but it will have to be lived by those who no longer are merely followers of that one, but who have become inspired by that one and are thereby encouraged to go and do likewise. There is no other way.

If, by our example or by our works, we could overcome all the disease and all the sin in any one city today, tomorrow there would be another crop of sick people and sinners. If we could walk through the hospitals today and heal every person there and walk through the prisons and release every prisoner, tomorrow those same rooms would be filled with other people. No matter how high we may go, individually, we are only an infinitesimal part of a story with an unhappy ending, *unless through our life others become illumined.*

It sounds like a very difficult task—and it is. It would seem that the amazing things we have been witnessing in this work for so many years should be awakening the world. But the world sleeps on—except for one here and one there, and another one here and another one there. And so it is that our function is not merely to receive this light and to bring about a few healings, but so to live that our lives inspire others to go and do likewise.

As the Spirit of the Lord, the Christ, finds outlet through your consciousness, It touches the lives of all those you meet on life's highway. In opening your consciousness to the activity of the Christ and by not restricting It or attempting to direct It, you permit It to escape into human consciousness and bring God's grace to those persons who open themselves to that Grace. You become an instrument through which the activity of the Christ can reach others in the world.

One person cannot do it for the world; one person cannot do it even for a community. It is only insofar as entire groups are spiritually prepared and willing to go out and continue to do the work which some one individual here or there has heretofore been doing and thereby multiply that work—not one by one, but a hundred times a hundred—that the light will penetrate the darkness of human consciousness, the dense materiality which resists everything in the nature of spiritual freedom.

The Responsibilities of Citizenship Must Be Accepted

You and I who have attained a degree of spiritual consciousness must be even more alert than other people to our obligations as citizens. This cannot be accomplished by adopting a do-nothing attitude of "What difference does it make who governs our country or what kind of men and women we have representing us in Congress or Parliament because they are all spiritual anyway?" That really is stupidity. True, we must maintain our own spiritual integrity by refraining from condemnation. This, however, is not to be construed as having no opinions.

It is certainly right to have opinions about governmental and world problems, but it is not right to be aggressively contentious about those opinions. As a matter of fact, we are perhaps more firmly established in our opinions if we have spiritual wisdom than would otherwise be the case. If we have a consciousness of man's true identity, the person who is peculiarly fitted for a particular position will be revealed to us in our meditations.

137

In other words, just as we are guided to one another as patients and practitioners, or as students and teachers, so are we guided to vote for the right candidate and the right party at any given time.

We should not shirk the responsibilities and privileges which citizenship entails. We render unto Caesar the things that are Caesar's, obeying the law of the land, paying taxes and performing services with which we may not always be in accord and which we sometimes may feel are entirely wrong, but even while we do those things and recognize the wrongness of them humanly, every student of spiritual wisdom can be about his special business of prayer and become a part of a world-wide activity to bring the realization of the kingdom of God to earth through uplifted consciousness. Even though humanly we are unimportant to the world and its governments, nevertheless we can be a greater power than those who sit in the seats of the mighty, because through our spiritual realization, we can help to settle the affairs of the world, not by might and not by power, but by the Spirit of God.

There has never been a time since the beginning of recorded history when the world has not used material force to gain its way and its will; and even today, with all the progress that has been made, the world has not yet learned that lasting victories are not won by means of material force. It has not learned that the battle may be won, but the war lost; that a particular war may be won, but far more lost than has been gained, often resulting in a repetition of the conflict on a larger and more violent scale. Very seldom does a war accomplish its purpose, except temporarily. Always the great powers have eventually gone down in defeat. It is inevitable. "For all they that take the sword shall perish with the sword."[1]

Those who have gone one step ahead in spiritual understanding, wherever they are and of whatever persuasion, must accept responsibility not only for their own community and nation, but for world conditions. The world grows increasingly smaller. It has become our community and everyone in it our neighbor. Today, almost any place in the world can be reached in twenty hours; next year or the year after, it may be ten. Do you not see that boundaries are becoming of less significance and importance in a world where mountains, rivers, and oceans are no longer barriers? Boundaries are artificial lines drawn by man in an attempt to divide the world into "mine" and "thine"; they are created by man who has forgotten that "the earth is the Lord's, and the fulness thereof"[2] and that he stands in relationship to that fulness as an heir.

When you travel 20,000 feet up in the air in an airplane and look down, you can really see and believe that the earth is the Lord's—just one great, big, round ball. Down here it seems natural to have a fence around some segment of this earth and assert possessively, "Don't come in here. This belongs to me"; but it looks foolish from 20,000 feet up in the air.

And so it is from a higher state of spiritual consciousness. From that state, it looks foolish to pray for your land or my land, for your people or my people,

[1] Matthew 26:52.   [2] Psalm 24:1.

because unless we see God as your Father and my Father, our prayers are useless. So let us not be concerned only about our own government, but let our concern embrace the whole world, that the spiritual Kingdom may be made humanly manifest. Let us realize that the government is upon His shoulders—the government of mankind, the government of the world, until we do come to that day when we realize: "This world is not governed by might or by power, but by the Spirit of the Lord."

If there are ten righteous men in the city, the city may be saved. In other words, there is no way to measure the degree of power which may flow through one individual consciousness, realizing the presence of God. Our faith is not in might or in power; our faith is not in the ballot, because that is merely the might of numbers or percentages: Our ultimate reliance is in the degree of our awareness of the presence of God and of our realization of the impersonal and universal nature of the Christ.

Not one of us has any idea who may be touched by the Christ through our realization and be in such a position that his influence can balance the scale on the side of spiritual power. We have no way of knowing who the individual is, or where, or when, who may be struck as Saul of Tarsus was struck with a blinding light and awakened out of his "Saul-ness" into "Paul-ness."

Encircling the World with a Band of Christ-Consciousness

It is not a person who will save the world: It is the Christ. The person in the right place at the right time, with a degree of receptivity, will be the one through whom It will appear to come. You and I, however, do not have to wonder who he is or where. We need only dwell in the realization that salvation will come, not by might, nor by power, but by the Spirit of God. Your function and mine is to be instruments through which the presence of God can touch and awaken humanity. It is our only reason for living.

When The Infinite Way was given to me, I visioned a band of Christ-consciousness around the world, so that every individual who reached out to God, regardless of his religion or lack of religion, would automatically find God with him. Work toward this end cannot be carried on by the general public, nor can it be carried on by people who are unwilling to sacrifice something of themselves for truth and for the establishment of the kingdom of God on earth. It can only be carried on by the dedicated people of the world.

Are you willing to count yourself among those dedicated and consecrated people who have risen above self-seeking and who think in terms of universality rather than personality? Are you willing to give periods of meditation every day to the dissolving of the material sense which holds the world in bondage? The Christ is hidden inside of you, but you must release that Christ into the world. Be willing to sit in the silence until you have a conscious feeling that God is on the field. Then the Christ is functioning. After you have achieved the awareness of the Christ, realize that this Christ is dissolving the errors of this world—dissolving material sense—and that that realization of the Christ is opening human consciousness to a receptivity to truth. Just to make the statement that human consciousness is being opened to truth is a waste of time, but to have realized the Christ and then to know that this realization of the Christ is operating in human consciousness to make it receptive to Truth will be effective.

In this meditation, you are not criticizing or condemning anybody; you are not judging as to whether material sense is operating in this one or in that one: You are realizing that wherever material sense raises its head, this realized Christ is dispelling it.

For your own unfoldment and that of your family, patients, and students, give as many meditation periods as possible for the purpose of renewing yourself in the Spirit of the Lord. But, in addition to that, give three periods out of every twenty-four hours to the world. This is your contribution to world freedom. Therefore, three times each day open out a way for the Spirit of the Lord God which is upon you to escape into the world.

Let your first meditation period be only for the purpose of feeling a consciousness of God's presence. When that has been achieved, that is the end of that period of meditation for the world. In your second meditation dedicated to world freedom, again achieve a conscious awareness of God's presence and realize that this realization of the Christ is dispelling material sense in human consciousness. Begin your third meditation once again with a realization of the Christ, and then recognize that that realization of the Christ is dispelling material sense and opening human consciousness to a receptivity to Truth.

That is your gift to the world—little enough to give for the priceless gift you have received. Through these meditations, you are admitting the Christ into human consciousness three times a day, thereby creating in humankind the desire for spirituality, a hunger and thirst for spiritual righteousness and freedom.

This realization of the Christ is already an activity of Infinite Way students all over the world. Out of the twenty-four hours of the day, there is not a single thirty minute period when, in some place or other, this work of realizing the Christ is not going on. It has been given to me that if a band of realized Christ-consciousness is formed around the world, it will touch and awaken individual consciousness and bring lasting freedom to the world.

Most of you have proved in your own experience that every time you have a realization of the Christ, some harmony comes to you or to those around you. The purpose of realizing the Christ, however, never has been solely to bless you or your family. The Christ is universal, and Its function is to establish the kingdom of God on earth. Therefore, Its activity is not limited to you or to me; It is not limited to a few favored persons: "For he maketh his sun to rise on the evil and on the good, and sendeth rain on the just and on the unjust."[1]

Humanly the problem of freedom has never been adequately solved, but in this work, we leave the human situation to those who are working on that

[1] Matthew 5:45.

plane in their own way, always remembering, if we live in free countries having free elections, to exercise our rights and duties as citizens. But let us put our dependence and reliance on prayer, on the realization that the Christ realized dissolves material sense and that It does operate in human consciousness to make it receptive to spiritual truth and to free it from the ignorance and superstition which have held it in bondage.

Then we shall see the world transformed. I, for one, am convinced that such a transformation can take place without bloodshed, without severe financial depressions, and without dividing the nations of men one against another, but by bringing them into a greater sense of fellowship. That cannot be done by fighting with bullets or with arguments: It can only be done by fighting with love, which is not fighting at all. It can only be accomplished by the realization of the Christ, by praying that the Christ be realized in individual consciousness. Then when our enemy has been touched by the Christ, he is no longer our enemy: He is our Self.

ACROSS THE DESK

There are not *many* evils in the world: There is only one evil. Sin, disease, death, lack, loneliness, homelessness, unemployment, war, epidemics, typhoons, and tempests—all these can be embraced in what Paul termed, "the carnal mind," and which is today often spoken of as "mortal mind" or "hypnotism." But inasmuch as the carnal or mortal mind is not the mind of God, it is not law, nor indeed can be; it is not life, power, being, or presence, and therefore can be dismissed as the "arm of flesh," or nothingness.

The Infinite Way reveals that there are no miracles to be demonstrated such as health, supply, home, employment, or the stilling of storms; but rather, there is only *one* miracle—the demonstration of God. When the awareness of the presence of God has been attained, the harmonies of God's grace flow like a river.

When this awareness of God's presence becomes realized consciousness among our students, they will do the greater works, but it is evident that up to this time their progress in spiritual healing has been far too slow. I have prayed about this for a long, long while, and in the past few weeks, it has occupied my periods of meditation both day and night, and finally it has been revealed to me why their progress is not more rapid.

Many, many times in classes, I have said that eventually healing will be accomplished with a smile, meaning by that that there is very little conscious effort necessary to bring about spiritual healing, and that when one attains a sufficiently high state of consciousness, healings come naturally, and often with startling rapidity. But it has come to me recently that our students feel that they can start right from the beginning with that very-little-effort state of consciousness, and for this reason, they are not accomplishing that which they have set out to do.

Now I am going to ask those of you who really and truly want to do more and better healing work— whether for your families and friends or whether you wish to accept calls from other students or eventually take up the serious practice of healing—to embark upon a program of earnest study and unremitting practice.

Go back to *The Infinite Way Letters of 1954*[1] through *1958*[2] and pick out the *Letters* pertaining to specific treatment work and specific principles of healing. For example, in November, 1955, the subject of *The Letter* was "Suggestions for Healing Work," and in that same year, there was another one on protective work. Throughout the years, there have been many *Letters* on these two subjects. Study all these *Letters* diligently, and always be sure to begin every day with the chapters, "The New Horizon," in *The Infinite Way*,[3] "Love Thy Neighbor," in *Practicing the Presence*,[4] and *The Letters* of December, 1958, and June, 1959.

What I am trying to point out is the necessity of understanding the specific principles that are to be taken into a treatment and the importance of bringing these principles to conscious remembrance in your treatment. Then, after having been very thorough in giving the treatment, take the attitude, "Speak, Lord; for thy servant heareth."[5] Wait for one, two, or three minutes, or four or five, until you feel that inner release, or "click." But that second

[1] By the author (Honolulu, Hawaii: Mercantile Printing Co., 1954).

[2] By the author (London, England: L. N. Fowler & Co., 1956, 1957, 1958, 1959).

[3] By the author (San Gabriel Calif.: Willing Publishing Co., 1947).

[4] By the author (New York: Harper & Brothers, 1958; London, England: L. N. Fowler & Co., 1958).

[5] I Samuel 3:9.

half of the treatment, which is the most important part as far as the healing work is concerned, will not be effective if the first half of the treatment has not been thorough and complete. It is true that, after two or three years of concentrated practice, gradually the first half of the treatment which is the application of these specific principles becomes shorter, and the second half of the treatment becomes the longer part.

Do not believe for a moment that you can avoid those first years of specific application of specific truths in treatment, for this is what develops consciousness. Through the correct letter of truth, the spiritual awareness of truth is attained. Of course, I realize that inertia is all that is keeping our students from faithfully doing this work. The human mind is lazy. People are always trying to find short cuts—anything that will eliminate the necessity for hard work. They prefer to go to the movies, watch television, and look at picture magazines, rather than to read a book.

To sit down, study, and meditate for several hours a day, and in the course of a day or evening give a dozen intelligent, complete treatments, covering the many different situations of life, is not an easy program; but then, the spiritual way of life is not an easy way of life, albeit a joyous one.

I truly believe that all of you who receive these *Letters* are sufficiently sincere in your devotion to God and to the service of mankind that you really want to develop a healing consciousness. I am sure that you have the capacity to do this, but I want to make it very clear that I have no way of giving it to you through any short cuts. It means work, it requires diligence, and it demands of you perseverance. The important thing is the amount of actual practice which you give to this work. It is true that an hour a day will eventually develop your consciousness and bring about the ability to heal, but at this time I have in mind a program which should occupy you for two, three, and four hours a day, at least that long for those of you who can manage to give this much time to the development of your consciousness.

There are those who, by the grace of God, receive spiritual illumination and healing power without going through all these years of preparation; but there are not many such, and there is no use believing that you are one of those few, unless the fruitage in your life already testifies to that fact. If you are not the instrument for many, many healings, and good healings, why fool yourself into thinking that you can have this gift without the hard work that goes before it?

CONSCIOUS DOMINION

To live the spiritual life means to give up personal sense and come into the understanding that we have no life of our own, but that that life which is ours is really God's life expressed as our individual life or experience. This is the truth about our life, but more than that, this is the truth about every individual on earth whether or not he knows it. In that realization, lies a principle which can be of the utmost importance in our relationships with one another.

If we are to give up the personal sense of life, we must learn to "die daily" to the old man, that man who has been living his own life, a life lived strictly in accordance with his own desires and for his own purposes. Although there is no doubt that many people have lived their own lives for very unselfish purposes, it does not necessarily follow that these lives were lived in accordance with spiritual law. Their very unselfishness may have carried with it a self-righteous, rigid attitude of being good humanly and doing good humanly. The spiritual life, however, is a recognition that "I can of mine own self do nothing,"[1] that man does not have the capacity to be either good or bad.

[1] John 5:30.

The World's Response to Us Is the Result
of Our Reaction to It

In our relationship with friends, family, and members of our community, we would soon notice what a difference there would be, if instead of forming dislikes or harboring resentments because people do not act as we think they should act, we were able to maintain our balance and spiritual equilibrium, realizing that man has no power to be right or wrong, to do the right thing or to do the wrong thing, because all power resides in God, the Soul of man, the life of man.

If, instead of reacting to those in our family who are consistently trying to take advantage of us, those who are unappreciative, ungrateful, thoughtless, and unkind, we were to lift ourselves above such suggestions and realize that there is no one in our home who can give or withhold good—no one in our family who can withhold recognition or co-operation—the whole situation would change.

As you apply this principle, you will discover something I learned in the healing work, and that is that the world's response toward me is the direct result of my own reaction to it. In other words, if someone calls and asks for help for an illness and I accept that as a reality and become fearful or doubtful or set about going to work diligently to overcome it, the reaction would be so strong that the healing would not take place very quickly. As a matter of fact, there would be no healing at all until I could rise above any reaction to the problem.

On the other hand, when a call comes, if I am sufficiently high in consciousness to respond with, "So what! What can it do! It has no power that it did not get from God! In and of itself, a mirage has no power to cover the road with water, and in and of itself, an illusion cannot do anything or be anything," and if that state of consciousness is my only reaction to the problem, the healing may be instantaneous, or at least it will be quick.

There must be the same reaction to injustice, unkindness, and ingratitude, always that sense of "What difference does it make? It hasn't anything to do with me. If there is any injustice, it is not directed toward me—it is directed toward the Christ, and the Christ can take care of it. If there is any ingratitude, it is not toward me—it is an ingratitude toward the Christ, and the Christ knows how to take care of that."

Rising Above Personal Sense

To take such an attitude is to eliminate the personal sense of "I." By "dying daily" to the personal sense of self, you no longer react to the world's fears, beliefs, condemnations, and aggravations; and therefore, you are aloof from them, and they do not inflict themselves upon you. Any demand that is made upon you is not made upon you, but upon the Christ of your being. Therefore, you have no right to react to it.

Always remember that the trials and tribulations of the world never come nigh the dwelling place of the person who dwells "in the secret place of the most High," who lives and moves and has his being in

God-consciousness. To be established in God-consciousness means to understand, first of all, that God is your consciousness, and therefore you never accept anything as personal to you, but let the God-consciousness of you take care of it; and secondly, that God is the consciousness of all being, and so if any discord or inharmony seems to come into your experience, you will understand that it is not from any person at all but from an illusory sense of him, which we call "man, whose breath is in his nostrils," and of him it says, "for wherein is he to be accounted of?"[1]

To come into this higher sense of life means to overcome the personal sense of life. In other words, it means to rise to a place in consciousness where "the fiery darts of the wicked"[2] no longer touch you. Even then, there is no guarantee that the world may not gossip or spread rumors about you, or that it may not fire bullets at you. It may do all those things, but the answer is always the same, "What difference does it make since the *I* of me is God, and that *I* can never be hurt?" As long as you live in the sense that only the qualities and activities of God can flow out from you, what difference does it make what the world does to you or to me?

The entire experience of the Crucifixion served as a proof that even the nails, the cross, and the sword had no power. Furthermore, it proved that neither the opposition and hatred of the organized church, nor the temporal pomp and glory of Rome were power. The Resurrection celebrated at Easter symbolizes that human hatred of truth is not power,

[1] Isaiah 2:22.   [2] Ephesians 6:16.

that the weapons of this world—its nails and swords —are not power, and that human law is not power. That is the great lesson to be drawn from the Crucifixion and the Resurrection. The Resurrection proved that whatever form of evil is thrust at us, "in three days," we can rise above it. In a short period of time, we can rise above any and every form of discord or inharmony if we not only do not accept it as a real power, but, moreover, do not accept it as being aimed at us as people, but really aimed at the Christ of our being, and then are willing to behold the Christ nullify it.

Wherever and whenever anyone is nursing resentment toward us, displaying jealousy, envy, or malice, engaging in cutthroat competition, or wherever there is the threat of temporal power or lack of appreciation, ingratitude, gossip, or rumor, the answer should always be the same:

It makes no difference. "Man, whose breath is in his nostrils" has no power of his own to do anything or to be anything, since God is the mind of man, and all power is centered in, and emanates from, God. Not one of the Pilates of this world has power over me, unless it comes from the Father in heaven.

When the children of Israel came crying to Hezekiah because of their fear of the great troops which were massing against them, he responded with calm assurance, "Be strong and courageous, be not afraid nor dismayed . . . With him is an arm of flesh; but with us is the Lord our God to help us."[1] In other words, the enemy had only temporal power and physical might. What was that to Hezekiah

[1] II Chronicles 32:7, 8.

and his people? They had the power of God.

Would it not be strange to have the power of God and yet to fear what man can do to us? We are told not to fear what mortal man can do: "The Lord is on my side; I will not fear: what can man do unto me?"[1] That should not be interpreted as meaning that we are sitting here with God, but that the enemy does not have God; it does not mean that we have a God here to defend us against somebody evil out there. No, it means that God is the only power; and with the understanding of God as the only power, God then becomes the only voice that can be heard.

There is no way on earth by which we can be convinced that evil is not power unless we can see that there is a God, that God is, and that that God that is, is the only power, and that that God is actually the law, principle, and substance of individual being. To believe that a God out here somewhere is love, truth, justice, and mercy is futile. This divine Principle is inoperative unless we understand that God is the principle of *individual being*, that God is the law and the substance and the activity of individual you and me, and of individual him and her.

Until you recognize God as individual being, until you can see God, not only as universal good, but universal good individually expressed, not only that God is universal infinite power, but universal infinite power individually expressed, only then can you look at any and every person and know, "The only power you have is to express God, or to let God

1 Psalm 118:6.

express Itself through you." Then when someone rises up and flauntingly boasts, "Look how great I am! I can crucify you," you smile because you know that God is the mind, the life, and the Soul of that particular person who has become the Pilate in your life and that he could not be empowered to do anything other than to let God flow.

The Pure in Heart Are
Untouched by Evil

No one can defy God, and more especially, no one can defy God once he comes up against someone who knows the truth. True, the sinner apparently seems to flourish for awhile, and evil institutions seem to dominate the human world. And why? Because there is no understanding of this principle. But let anyone try evil machinations against a person of pure mind, and you will soon see not only that his power of evil is destroyed, but that if he does not mend his ways he eventually destroys himself. Evil always runs rampant until it hits up against the pure in heart.

This point is well illustrated in the case of the hypnotist who was trying to entertain the members of a family of metaphysicians by hypnotizing them and who found that he not only could not hypnotize anyone in the group, but when, in a final attempt to display his wares, he decided to hypnotize his wife with whom he had always succeeded heretofore, he found that he could not even hypnotize her. He had hit up against the pure in heart—those who were consciously aware of but one mind and one power operating in that room. That nullified the belief that one person had a mind that could be used over another person. As long as everybody in the room believed that there were two minds, the group could be hypnotized; but when one person came along who had a sufficiently strong conviction that there was only one mind in the room, a mind which could not be destructive to itself, then the hypnotist could not operate successfully.

So it will be in your individual experience and mine when we become pure of heart, which means the moment we arrive at the conviction that God is the mind of each one of us and that not one of us has qualities or activities separate or apart from the activity of that one mind, and that no other mind is operating and no other mind can operate. Only the qualities and activities which emanate from the one mind are expressing and those are qualities of intelligence, qualities of love and life, qualities of pure being. Then should there be someone in our experience who might attempt to hypnotize or harm us, his attempts would be nullified, and he would have no power over us.

Let us individually become pure of mind, that is, come to the realization of God as individual mind, life, and Soul. Then only the qualities of God can flow out from us to the world. Let us behold the Christ sitting between the eyes of every individual; let us behold only the Christ as the substance and law of every condition; and then there will be no duality in our consciousness, and no duality can return to us.

By that realization we make ourselves an avenue for the outflowing of good, but we do more than that.

By realizing the universality of that truth, we prevent any evil from coming nigh our dwelling place. In other words, we nullify the activity of evil in the individual as did Jesus in Pilate, "Thou couldest have no power at all against me, except it were given thee from above."[1]

You will find that as you diligently pursue this idea, you will never again look to "man, whose breath is in his nostrils" for anything. That does not mean that if you want some help you will not ask for it from a practitioner. Certainly, you can do that, but actually you would not be expecting the help from a person, although you would expect it to come through him as the activity of divine Love.

No Power Apart from God Can Act upon You

No matter what befalls you in the outer world, you come to this agreement and acknowledgment, "Only the activity of divine Wisdom is power." You cannot talk about the allness of God and the allness of God's power, and then ask, "I wonder why I do not get this healing; I wonder what power is operating in this situation besides God; I wonder what is holding me back." Do you see how impossible such an attitude becomes if you catch the truth of God's allness? Some change must take place in your thought and actions the moment you become convinced that there is no power apart from God and that man has no power over you.

You cannot blame the stars and say that they have power over you, because God made the stars and the planets, so they must also be avenues

[1] John 19:11.

through which good operates in your experience. There is no use attributing your problems to your birth date, to your horoscope, or to the lines of your palm. God made the lines of your palm and they must be avenues for the expression of good. God made all that was made.

Bit by bit, you begin to withdraw power from man, first, by developing the ability to see that man cannot give you anything and that man cannot withhold anything from you. You are receptive and responsive only to God-government. Only the one mind is the law unto your being. Then why hold anybody else responsible for your troubles? What is the use of blaming anybody for having given you too much or for not having given you enough, when the actual truth is that God is the law unto your being and God is the life and the love of your being? If you have looked to anybody else, it has been your fault. You have put your faith in princes, so why should you blame someone else for having betrayed you when you had no right to look to him in the first place? God alone should have been your reliance and your dependence.

The second thing that takes place in your experience is that you begin to withdraw power from things, circumstances, and conditions. Nothing from outside has power over you or over your affairs. For example, if you are driving on the highway, you should understand that the life which is God is not at the mercy of stupidity, carelessness, or indifference—none of these things is power. Granted that on the human level of consciousness there is such a thing as stupidity; granted that there is such a thing as carelessness or drunken driving. But even if these things do exist, are they power? Can they have power over the life which is God, and is there any other life? Can they have power over the mind or body of God? Is there any mind or body other than God? Has any person any other mind than that of God? Are those human qualities of indifference or carelessness, which seem to be operating through him, power?

You can apply this principle to every form of life —snakes, sharks, poisonous insects. You can apply it to anything there is in the world—infection, contagion, germs—by asking yourself the question, "If God made all that was made, are these things outlets or avenues for anything other than God?"

If you have entertained an evil sense of some person or condition, in this moment of dedication, purify yourself of such beliefs. In all this world, there is not an evil person or condition that has within itself any power of evil. Regardless of what it may be, regardless of how venomous or deadly its appearance may be at this moment, you will remove its sting, its seemingly destructive nature, if you can look upon the person or condition with this conviction:

You have no powers of evil, for there are none. I have mislabeled you, and the world has mislabeled you, when it claims that you are evil, dangerous, or destructive. I know that it is not true, because I know that in all the universe there is no person or thing or condition that has any quality of evil in it, any power of evil, or any power of destruction. There is only God.

If I walk "through the valley of the shadow of death,

I will fear no evil,"[1] *because there is no evil in that condition. Though I seem to be consumed by disease, I will no longer fear it, for it has within itself no element of destruction, no element of pain, no element of death. It is in and of itself nothingness, since all power is in God.*

I will not judge by appearances, but I will withhold all judgment as to good or evil and stand fast in the realization that God alone is good. Even this that I have been hating is not evil; even this about which I have been wondering as to why or how it could intrude into my dwelling place, I now know is not evil—it has no qualities of evil, and he or she has no qualities of evil.

Nothing is good, nothing is evil: All that is, is of God, and therefore spiritual—above quality, above quantity. In the realm of God, there is neither quality nor quantity: There is only infinity, eternality, immortality—a divine state of being which has no opposites, no good and no evil, but only pure spiritual being.

God's allness and God's goodness and God's power and God's law permeate me, this universe, all being, and all conditions.

The miracles of Grace come into your experience in proportion as you withdraw all labels from the world of men and women, from conditions, things, and circumstances, and no longer speak a language of comparisons, but recognize God as the creative Principle of all, and therefore all as spiritual.

Your Consciousness Is the Law unto Your Experience

You will never again be able to blame a person, circumstance, or a condition for the inharmonies of your life, because you will recognize that it is nothing

[1] Psalm 23:4.

that goes *into* your experience that defileth or maketh a lie, nothing that "man, whose breath is in his nostrils" can do to you, but rather it is what emanates from your own consciousness that is the law unto your experience.

This is in no sense a denial of the fact that in our human experience we, and the rest of the world, are daily being faced with the same evils that have always plagued mankind and which, instead of decreasing, seem to be increasing. To free ourselves of the evils that beset us and then to help others attain their freedom is the goal of The Infinite Way.

We attain this freedom through the revelation given to us that all of the world's evils, from the beginning of time unto the end of all time—those that affect us individually, nationally, and universally—must be recognized as the emanation or expression of what Paul called the "carnal mind," what metaphysics has termed "mortal mind," and which the Bible has described as the "fleshly mind"; but then we must take the next and final step which is that this mind of evil is not mind because it is not God-created and has no law of God to sustain it. What sets us free is the impersonalization of evil and the understanding that it exists only as temporal power or the "arm of flesh" and, therefore, is no power.

It was Jesus who said, "Not that which goeth into the mouth defileth a man; but that which cometh out of the mouth, this defileth a man."[1] In that one statement of the Master's, the whole responsibility

[1] Matthew 15:11.

161

is placed where it belongs—not what goes into the mouth, not what goes into the mind, not what goes into you, but what comes out. There is your responsibility. That is what lifts you above the puppet-like lot of the ordinary human being and makes you master of your fate and captain of your own Soul. That is determined, not by words, but by the conviction maintained in consciousness. Do you believe that "man, whose breath is in his nostrils" or the "princes" of this world can give you anything? Do you believe that they can withhold anything or take anything from you? If you do, that is what is coming out of your consciousness, and that is what corrupts, defiles, and makes your whole life-experience one of disappointment and failure. It is all dependent on what you entertain in consciousness.

Any inability to be master of your life-experiences, at least for those occurring before you came into truth, stems from your failure to assume conscious dominion over your life because then you were living in ignorance of the principles of life which give you mastery over circumstances and conditions. For example, to believe in the power of infection, contagion, or germs, to believe in the inevitability of accidents or in accidents as an act of God, or to believe in any destructive influence at all is merely the result of ignorance. You were born into those beliefs, brought up with them, and those beliefs became your master, so that if you sat in a draft, you were bound to catch cold because you had to follow the established pattern of reaction, and if you were out on the highway and encountered a reckless driver, almost certainly you would get hurt. None of that was your fault: It was due to your ignorance of spiritual law.

The moment, however, that you taste of spiritual wisdom, the whole situation changes. You can no longer be duped by mass ignorance, nor be victimized by it. You now know what the law is and that the principle is God's allness and the nothingness of anything else claiming to be power. In proportion as you place power in any person, in that degree can that person exercise power over or against you. In proportion as you realize that all power is in God, the mind and Soul of the individual, then the only power any person can exercise over you is that power which emanates from God. You are the controller of what happens to you, not the people in your home, your social set, community, or world.

If you believe that you are the victim of some person's ingratitude or the beneficiary of another person's gratitude, you make yourself responsive to those very things. If you believe that you are the beneficiary of some kind, benevolent, and philanthropic person's goodness, but also the victim of another person's wickedness, you lay that law upon yourself, because whatever comes out of your consciousness determines what will be the law in your experience, whether of discord or harmony, and it will maintain or destroy the integrity of your existence:

No man or woman has the power of good or of evil in my experience. The only power there is, is in and of God which is individual mind, life, Soul, and consciousness. Therefore, every person I meet is an avenue of good in my experience.

There are some people who will not permit

163

themselves to be avenues for good in your experience, regardless of the measure of your realization, but those people are eventually removed from your experience to a place where they cannot exercise any power for evil over you. Those who come into your experience with negative qualities are either healed or removed.

Spiritual Selectivity in Relationships

When we walk this spiritual path, we find that people either walk with us or are led away from us. You can prove this if, at the end of one, two, three, or five years, you cast a backward glance on the friends or enemies of yesteryear. Where are those friends you had but a few years ago? Many have disappeared out of your life. You did nothing to get rid of them; they were just naturally eliminated. This does not mean that disaster overtook them. On the contrary, they may have made progressive strides forward in their world, according to their own standards of progress, but they could not or did not care to walk your path, and so your ways separated.

However, at the same time this separation from former associates has been going on, you have most likely been attracting to yourself those of your spiritual household, those who were of your own state of consciousness, and while you may have far fewer friends than you had before, the quality of those friendships will more than compensate for the quantity. The friends you have attracted to yourself on your upward spiritual march are so completely in that same God-consciousness that they fulfill every need of your experience. You do not need numbers. Numbers are unimportant. One, two, or three of such spiritually attuned friends can fulfill a person's life on the spiritual plane, although he may still have large numbers of what the world calls acquaintances.

We must stop this looking outside of ourselves to people and complaining, "What are you doing to me?" And at the same time we must remember that the goodness and kindness of people is God shining through. Jesus said, "Why callest thou me good? there is none good but one, that is, God."[1] That is a principle of harmony in our life, but it can only benefit us in proportion as we adopt it as a principle in our experience and live it: "From now on, I will not be resentful of those who despitefully use me, persecute or abuse me. I will not be resentful of those who lie and cheat and defraud. I will not be resentful of those who are ungrateful or unsatisfying in any way, shape, manner, or form, because I know now that no person has the will or the power to do evil, and when an individual appears to be the instrument for evil that is but the carnal mind. I have taken the name of God and realize God to be my true identity, and if God is my true identity, can my good come from anywhere except from within myself?"

Do you begin to see how the entire success or failure of your life has its foundation in you—not in what others do to you or in what others refrain from doing for you? You have the power within yourself to establish a successful and harmonious life.

[1] Matthew 19:17.

The principle is that regardless of what you think your wife, husband, child, parent, employer, or employee is doing to you, you must make your conscious oneness with this principle in this realization:

"I and my Father are one." [1] *The activity of God, or truth, in my consciousness is the only law unto my being, and it will heal or remove anything or anybody that is opposed to Its spiritual activity.*

Can you rise high enough to live this principle? Will you make it a matter of daily realization?

God is my true identity: God is the source of my supply, the source of my satisfaction, the source of my income, and God is the source of my business, my home, my safety, and my security. Hid with Christ in God, what danger can come nigh my dwelling place? If God is my sanctuary, my strength, and fortress, then I have only to rest in the realization of God as my being. I live, move, and have my being in God, and no evil can come nigh my dwelling place because of my realization of God as my true identity.

It is not the function of anybody in the world to provide me with an income, with safety, security, activity, customers, patients, or students. That all must take place as the activity of God at the center of my being because everything takes place within me. Then this truth that I know goes out and makes the crooked places straight, draws unto me my own, and separates me from those who have no right to be a part of my spiritual household.

The consciousness of truth within me becomes the law of my life and the law unto all those who bring themselves to me.

[1] John 10:30.

Up to this time, I have purposely avoided pinpointing the specific healing principles of The Infinite Way and instead have embodied them in the Writings so that students would gradually assimilate them as their spiritual capacities were unfolded and enlarged. Paul tells us clearly that the reasoning mind cannot know God, or Truth, or even be subject unto It. It is therefore necessary that students evolve spiritually before they can receive, understand, and demonstrate spiritual principles.

During the early years of my healing practice, two principles were revealed to me, which are not incorporated in the modern healing religions, but which were fully known to Moses, Buddha, and Christ Jesus. The revelation of these healing principles made possible those successful years during which my life was devoted to the active healing practice and eventually they led to the further revelations which constitute the message of The Infinite Way.

It is now evident that there are several hundred students sufficiently far along in the study and practice of the principles of The Infinite Way to be ready for further instruction in these specific healing principles and for their application in treatment and healing work. My work since April 8, when I was instructed to begin this teaching, has been preparing the way for this experience.

As students, your preparation for this experience is the *study and practice* of the chapter, "Protection," in *The 1955 Infinite Way Letters*[1]; the December 1958 and June 1959 *Letters*, and the chapter, "Love Thy Neighbor," in *Practicing the Presence*.[2]

Practice daily the giving of treatments embodying the principles found in these particular writings, and then follow up that work with the *study* and *practice* of Reels 5 and 6 of the 1959 Maui Advanced Work and Reels 3 and 4 of the 1959 Hawaiian Village Open Class. Above all, be sure that these principles come alive in you and that you develop a facility in applying specific principles in your meditation and treatment work.

Further work on the specific principles of healing will follow in the class work in Hawaii in July; San Diego, California, in August; London and Manchester, England, in September; The Hague, Holland, and Lausanne, Switzerland, in October; and in New York City in November.

Watch carefully for the two specific principles which constitute the major factor in spiritual healing work. You may be assured that I will make these clear to you, and this will enable you immediately to have confidence in your healing work and complete assurance that any problem that may arise in your experience can be met without question. The main requirement for you is the preparation of consciousness for the assimilation and understanding of these two principles, because without this preparation, the principles will be meaningless to you.

[1] By the author (London, England: L. N. Fowler & Co. Ltd., 1956).
[2] By the author (New York: Harper and Brothers, 1958; London, England: L. N. Fowler & Co., 1958).

THE IMPERSONALIZATION OF GOOD AND EVIL

MANY years ago the revelation was given to me that error is entirely impersonal: There is actually no such thing as an evil man or woman—there never has been and there never will be. When this revelation came to me in the early years of my practice, I saw that by impersonalizing error in every form, the burden was immediately lifted from me and from all those who came to me for help.

Perhaps there are not many men or women in full possession of their faculties who believe that they have always lived up to their highest standard of right, and certainly there are few people who do not carry a burden of guilt, even though few of them have committed theft, adultery, or any other act which the world classifies as a major sin. Everyone, however, has been guilty of not loving God supremely and of not loving his neighbor as himself, that is, of not doing unto others as he would have them do unto him.

Regardless of the depth of sin there may have been in your experience, or which may even be there now, "there is therefore now no condemnation,"[1] for in truth this sin is not of you. If you believed that these sins of omission or commission were your fault, do

[1] Romans 8:1.

you not see how you might be weighted down with a burden of guilt so great that you could never hope to rise above it? Instead of condemning yourself, be quick to recognize that what you have done or left undone was not your fault, but really your ignorance of how to prevent your doing these things. Sin is an impersonal, universal condition, based originally on the belief in two powers, good and evil, presented in its many and varied forms.

The realization of this for yourself or for your patients or students immediately lifts a weight from your and their shoulders. However, in no sense should this be interpreted as open permission to go out and repeat the offense. The Master always indicated that while he did not condemn sinners, they must go and sin no more.

Throughout all the writings of The Infinite Way, you will find this principle of the impersonalization of good and evil set before you for your assimilation and demonstration. At this point it should be helpful for you to go back and read those passages dealing with the impersonal nature of good and evil and seriously begin to put these principles into practice.

Recognize the Impersonal Nature of Evil

Understand that you are never to personalize error; you are never to look upon anyone as a sinner or to regard any person as the source of any form of evil, but immediately lift the condemnation from the person and realize, "No, this is not a person. This is that universal sense of evil, the carnal mind." Whether sin tempts us in one way or another—in the form of greed, lust, mad ambition, or some form of personal sense indulgence—it is but a sense of sin which comes to us for acceptance or rejection. In our unenlightened state, seeing only the appearance, we may judge of one, "You are a killer," of another, "You are a thief," of another, "You are an adulterer," or of yet another one, "You are disagreeable"; and in doing this we are bearing false witness against our neighbor because God is our neighbor.

From the moment we recognize that all error is impersonal, we never again blame a person—not even ourselves—for any form of evil, remembering that every form of evil is as impersonal as every form of good. Furthermore, never can we take credit for being good, just, benevolent, moral, honest, loyal, or faithful. Whatever of such qualities we possess are God-qualities and represent God expressing Itself as our individual qualities, characteristics, and nature. Whatever evil may be expressing itself through us at any given moment is the degree in which we are accepting the carnal mind as power, and either ignorantly or carelessly permitting it to function in us.

The Master said, "Ye shall know the truth, and the truth shall make you free."[1] We have to know the truth *consciously*, and, until the carnal mind is completely dead in us, we have to know it *constantly*. This, however, does not mean to set up two powers and begin protecting ourselves from one of them or fearing one of them. The carnal mind is not something to be fought, overcome, risen above, or destroyed: It is to be recognized as a nothingness, the "arm of flesh"—never personal.

[1] John 8:32.

If we personalize error in any form, we become the victim of it and are the blind leading the blind. That is why it is incorrect practice to admonish a patient or student, "You must be more loving," or, "You must be more forgiving," or, "You must be more grateful." Making such statements is personalizing the error.

If we find that a patient is not loving, kind, or gentle, that is, is not spiritual, then let us relieve that patient of the burden by realizing, "These negative qualities are not personal. They are part of the carnal mind, and the carnal mind is a nothingness."

If a patient says, "Oh, my trouble is hatred," or if the practitioner explains, "I have discerned that you are too full of hatred and malice," the error has been fastened to the individual so securely that healing becomes an impossibility. On the other hand, if we do detect these undesirable qualities, then let us quickly recognize them as a sign that this individual is being handled by that universal, or carnal, mind which forms itself in that particular way, but which is a nothingness, and therefore, because of its very nothingness, it cannot use the child of God as an avenue, as a channel, or as an instrument. The fact of its nothingness gives it no presence, no power, and no law with which to sustain its activities.

Separate the Error from Your Patient

This same principle applies to the problem of disease. It is not a person who is diseased, although he may be entertaining a sense of disease. Break the mesmerism by the realization that there is no disease: No person is diseased; no condition is diseased. Disease is a false sense: It is not a person, and no person has a disease. In this way, you separate the disease from your patient or student. Then you will be able to nullify it as a belief, an appearance, an illusion, as hypnotic suggestion, or as any of these terms which for you mean the "arm of flesh," or nothingness.

This principle can also be applied to a condition of lack and limitation. How could a person lack anything if he is joint-heir with Christ in God, as the Bible states? In our true identity, we are all joint-heirs to all the heavenly kingdom. That, however, does not alter the fact that we may be entertaining a sense of lack, unemployment, or unhappiness. But why entertain such a negative sense? Why not reject it by understanding, "This is not I and this is not mine. This is a universal sense coming to me for acceptance or rejection. Because it is not of God, I can easily reject it. Anything that God did not make was not made."

It makes no difference whether the something that presents itself to you is in the form of sin, disease, death, lack, limitation, or erroneous traits of character, you have the right and the responsibility to realize that the error is not personal, but a false universal sense presenting itself to you for acceptance or rejection, something which you can reject because it is not of God and, therefore, has no existence as reality or condition. Furthermore, because it is not of God, it has no law to sustain it. All that God made—and only that which God made—is sustained by law, by a spiritual law, the law of God, Spirit.

Whatever the picture presented to you, or whenever, you can immediately recognize it as a temptation to accept a false sense flowing from the universal mind, which is a nothingness and powerless to create anything. The universal mind can only present pictures or appearances. At the present stage of your unfoldment, this realization should come to you with the force and power of a recognized, definite principle for continuous moment-to-moment practice.

The Christ Cannot Be Finitized

There is a second part of this principle which is even more difficult to practice. Just as evil cannot be personalized, so good cannot be personalized. We now know that it is incorrect to say that anyone is a sinner, but it is equally incorrect to say that anyone is spiritual. Let us not make the futile attempt to pin Christhood to any person's humanhood or to any part of a person that is visible or tangible to sense. If there is any quality of good flowing through him, it is not his personal quality. It is a God-quality for which he is but the instrument.

We have learned that any evil quality which flows through an individual is not of himself, but is really a universal mesmerism which he has not consciously rejected. Now we must realize that if love, charity, benevolence, forgiveness, kindness, and co-operativeness are flowing through us, we must be careful not to take the credit for these qualities, for they do not have their source in us. We are but the instrument through which, and as which, God appears, the instrument through which good appears.

When we are called upon for help, we do not attempt to make a bad human being good, a poor human being rich, or a sinful person pure, but we turn immediately to the realization of the Christ. Note this point carefully: We do not try to add the Christ to a person, because the Christ cannot be finitized or personalized. The Christ is infinite, the son of God, which you are and which I am, but never can we finitize It or personalize It. Do not try to fasten your realization of the Christ onto a person, or direct It to a person, or send It out to a person, or believe that a person is It.

This is a very difficult point, but one which is absolutely essential to the healing work: Do not pin any form of error onto your patient, but neither pin any form of good onto him. When you sit down for treatment, there is nothing wrong or incorrect about having a momentary realization such as, "Well, I'm giving a treatment to Bob," but then let that be the end of any thought about Bob or whoever your patient is. From then on, do not even think of the patient; drop the patient completely from your thought. Turn to a realization of the Christ, but remember that the realization of the Christ will not come if you persist in keeping your patient uppermost in your mind. In the same way, when you sit down to give a treatment for your cat, dog, or bird, or the crop of berries in your garden, or the fruit on your trees, do not try to visualize the Christ as residing in these things, because that would be merely trying to finitize that which cannot be limited, and any such attempts could only result in failure.

Let me illustrate how this operates: If I receive a call for help from Mrs. Jones, I sit down to give her help; but the minute I go into meditation, I forget Mrs. Jones and turn within to the kingdom of God for a realization of the Christ. From within me will come some kind of an unfoldment, and that will be the healing agency. But whatever the nature of the unfoldment may be, I will not be trying to localize or limit it to Mrs. Jones.

"Then," you may ask, "how does Mrs. Jones receive the help?" And the answer is really a paradox. Mrs. Jones receives the help because in my meditation I have known that there is no Mrs. Jones: Mrs. Jones represents only a finite sense of being in my mind. When I am thinking about Mrs. Jones, I am entertaining a finite sense of the Christ because actually there is no Mrs. Jones: There is only the Christ—the Christ appearing to me erroneously as Mrs. Jones.

You might as well try to hold up an imaginary picture in your mind and attempt to heal it as to keep your thought on a Mrs. Jones, a Mrs. Brown, or a Mrs. Smith. To keep in your mind a finite picture that has been presented to you as a person, and then try to spiritualize that person is the same as trying to heal, reform, or enrich a mental picture. Do not do that.

When you receive a call, "Give me help," and you respond with, "I will be with you instantly"; you must immediately drop the patient, know the specific truth about the claim, recognize it as the activity of the carnal mind, and turn within to the center of your being that God may reveal to you His beloved Son—and that will be the Christ. You will meet with success as long as you do not try to fasten this Christhood onto a finite person.

Never Accept a Human Being into Your Consciousness to Be Healed

In your work as a spiritual healer, both the impersonalization of evil and the impersonalization of good are vitally important because otherwise you will merely be in another form of *materia medica*, trying to patch up a sick human being, and then next week having another sick person to change into a well one, until, if some of these patients remain with you long enough, you will one day have an old one wanting to be changed into a young one. Do not accept a human being into your consciousness.

If you are in this work long enough, you will have patients in their nineties, and you will feel just as responsible for their healing as if they were twenty-one, because you will not find it in your heart to believe that they are ever old enough to be senile, deaf, blind, or dead. But if you persist in taking human beings into your treatment and trying to spiritualize them, you will reach a time when helping them is an impossibility.

It is hardly necessary for me to remind you that if you were called upon to help some of the political leaders of the world, you might have a very difficult time trying to realize certain ones as the Christ of God, because the picture presented to you would be so contrary to Christhood. But if you are performing your spiritual function properly, you will have a period every day in which you realize that Christ is the government of every nation, that the government is upon His shoulders, not upon the shoulders of "man, whose breath is in his nostrils," and then you will have the vision of the Christ as the source of all government. But this cannot happen if you try to bring even a good leader into your meditation and attempt to pin Christhood onto him as a person. That will fail.

To behold the Christ is to lose sight of human beings, of humanhood, and to bear witness to the invisible Christ which I am and which you are: *I* am invisible. We have never seen each other; we have only seen our concept, or the world's concept, of our body. But *I*, we have not seen, for *I* am hiding behind the eyes.

If, in your meditation, you have asked, "What is this mystery of my true identity? Who am I? What am I? Why is it that I have always thought I was either this body or in this body and that some day in death I would leave this body?" sooner or later God will reveal to you the secret of the *I*—how you exist, where and when, and why *I* is not in a body, and never was, and never can be encompassed in a body.

And then you will know why I tell you so often, "Thou art the Christ, the son of the living God—not the you that people see with their human sight, but *Thou*, the *I* that you are, that which is invisible." That is why I cannot visualize It; that is why I cannot know what you look like or what your form is. Merely by looking out from a human standpoint,

I do not know what your character or nature is; but in my meditation, when I retire into the *I* that I really am, I can see you as you are, and can commune with you. Although I cannot see you with my eyes, nevertheless I know you: I can tabernacle with you and talk with you even though you may be 10,000 miles away, because the *I* of me is Omnipresence. Where *I* am, you are; wherever you are, *I* am; for *I* am in you, and you are in me, and we are one in God.

Omnipresence is the word, the omnipresence of *I*: *I* am here and *I* am there, and *I* am everywhere; *I* am within and *I* am without, for *I* am Omnipresence. When I forget your humanhood, then I can tabernacle with your spiritual Selfhood because spiritually we are one.

If, however, I were to try to credit the virtues of Christhood to your humanhood, I would fail. But as long as I understand the *I* of my true identity to be invisible, incorporeal, and omnipresent, I know that that is the truth about you, even if I cannot draw a picture of it—and that I cannot do. So it is that when you are thinking of your cat, your dog or bird, your berry patch or your fruit trees, your patients or your students, do not try to visualize them as spiritual. Spirituality is their true identity, but do not finitize it, do not try to picture it, and do not try to localize the Christ in a person.

No Mental Interference in Spiritual Healing

Furthermore, never try to send your thought out to a person, for then you are only indulging in a form of mental telepathy. In your meditation, do not attempt to enter the thought of your patients or students. That would be mental interference. On the human plane, a person with good motives and intentions can help someone with the power of thought, that is, with the power of his mind; but on the other hand, there is just as much possibility of the misuse of those powers, and that is where witchcraft and sorcery come in. Never attempt to enter the mind of your patients or students, because you are not functioning on the human plane of the mind. What you must do is to tabernacle with God within your own consciousness; and when you do that, then there is a spiritual bond between you and your patients and students which has in it nothing of a personal or finite nature.

If you follow the teaching of The Infinite Way, you will never mentally interfere with anyone because in this teaching the power of the mind is not used except as an avenue of awareness to remind ourselves of the correct letter of truth. This, you do not put into your patient's mind, nor do you project your thought to him. Over and over and over, I warn students against such incorrect practice. Do not project your thought to your patient and never use the words "you," "he," "she," or "it." When you are knowing the truth, know it within yourself and do not allow your mind to rove into any other person's domain, because that would be personalizing the error.

Give all the treatments you want to give, but give them to yourself. Realize and remember all the truth you can, until you arrive at that place where your thought quiets down and you need no more thought. Then let the Spirit of God talk to you, and the Christ will encompass everything necessary.

Never believe that it is your function to stray into the personal life, and certainly not into the mentality, of your patients or your students. When anyone reaches out to me for help, he is not a part of my human thought, and my human thought never becomes a part of him. I abide within myself, awaiting the realization of God's presence, and let the fact that he has reached out to me for help be the connecting link. No human thought of mine does that.

In my inner work, never do I indulge in human thought and never have I given a treatment to anybody. The treatment is always a realization of the truth. My work is directed to me, within myself, so that I know the truth of Being, thereby reminding myself of Omnipresence, of Oneness, of the one Power, the one Presence, the one Law, the one Life; and then I wait until the presence of God is upon me, and after that, those who have reached out for help feel it.

As long as you are not using truth for any personal gain or personal power, or in order to gain dominion over anyone, and as long as you are not permitting your thought to go out to your patient, you are abiding in the principles of The Infinite Way. The Infinite Way is not a mental science. The only treatment it knows is self-treatment. Treatment is only for the purpose of lifting yourself up to where you can reach a point in consciousness in which you can release the letter of truth and wait for the Spirit of God to do the work. Then you will be a blessing to everyone, because you are neither holding anyone in condemnation, nor are you trying to use anyone or to benefit yourself at his expense.

The Significance of Ananias and Sapphira

Any attempts to use truth for personal gain lead ultimately to one's own destruction. For awhile individuals do seem to benefit at another's expense, but in the end they pay dearly for it, sometimes in the loss of their lives or their sanity, but always in the loss of their particular form of activity.

To the pure all things are pure, and therefore anyone who tries to harm the consciousness that is spiritually pure, suffers a rebound from it that knocks him off his feet. In other words, your protection lies in your spiritual purity. This is illustrated in the story of Ananias and Sapphira. You remember that when the Master had ascended, the disciples were in a confused and chaotic state of mind, not knowing which way to turn or what to do. Temporarily they agreed to have a kind of communal society. They were living underground, persecuted by the church and unable to earn a living, and, therefore, in order to pool their resources, each one agreed to sell all that he had and turn the proceeds into a common fund.

As the head of the project, Peter took the responsibility of seeing that everybody was supplied with food, housing, and clothing, all of which was to be taken out of this general fund, and everyone did this except Ananias and Sapphira, who held back a little of what they had. When Peter discerned their unwillingness to share completely, he rebuked them: "Thou has not lied unto men, but unto God"[1] —you have not sinned against man: You have sinned against God. And Ananias and Sapphira dropped dead. The very moment that Peter impersonalized the error and said, in substance, "You did not rob me. Yours is an offense against God," the error rebounded to the persons guilty of it.

The impersonalization of both good and evil will make it impossible for anybody to harm you. Therefore, be careful that you do not personalize evil, even when someone tries to wrong you. Hold fast to the truth that he has not done this to you: He has done it unto God. And let God handle it. "Vengeance is mine; I will repay, saith the Lord."[2] That does not mean that there is a God who punishes people, but it means that when divine principles are violated, the violation destroys the one who violates them. God does not do this: The violation of the principle does it. When you think $2 \times 2 = 5$, mathematics does not harm you, but your violation of the principle of mathematics can work havoc with your finances. So it is that you cannot violate spiritual principles when you are on the spiritual path and succeed, more especially if you are mingling with those who understand this principle.

To the pure all things are pure, and as long as you remain in your spiritual integrity, the evils of this world will not come nigh your dwelling place. A thousand may fall at your left, and ten thousand at your right hand, but it will not come nigh you. Your function is neither to bless man mentally nor to curse man mentally, but to leave man strictly

[1] Acts 5:4. [2] Romans 12:19.

alone, and to realize within yourself God's grace and God's presence, and let those who have come to you and made themselves one with you be blessed by the presence of God—not by your mental jugglery, but by your concrete realization of the presence of God.

Anyone who brings himself to your consciousness benefits by your living in the conscious awareness of God's presence. When you approach the consciousness of such an enlightened person, you feel the actual presence of God. Let no one believe that any injury can come to any person living in the consciousness of God's presence.

Dwell in the conscious realization of God's presence and then everyone who has brought himself to your consciousness will feel It, for It is a presence, It is a power, It is a light, It is a law, It is a peace that passes understanding.

Across the Desk

Last August, I returned from Holland with inner instructions to cancel the remaining lecture and class work which had been arranged for the balance of 1958 in order to remain quietly at home and receive the work which was to be given next. At every step of the way in my work, I have received specific instructions, not only as to where to travel and when—and when not to travel, too—but instructions as to the nature of the message which was to be carried.

At the very beginning of my ministry, I was directed not to advertise for students, not to proselyte, and not to use human means for seeking supply, because the Spirit which gave me The Infinite Way would fulfill Itself in every avenue of activity—and it has proved to be so. Moreover, there has always been an awareness of an over-shadowing Presence. Twice, I have been warned inwardly of impending danger in air flights, but with each warning came the assurance that harmony would be established, and in both cases it was so.

Actually, the ultimate aim of The Infinite Way is to enable every student to make direct, *conscious* contact with the Source, so that each one may be so governed, guided, directed, and protected. It is the purpose of this Message to bring this spiritual Presence and Power to the conscious awareness of every student, and the study and practice of the specific principles which constitute The Infinite Way are the means of attaining the realization and demonstration of this spiritual consciousness.

Now I am ready to embark upon a trip which I look upon as as great an adventure as my first trip to England with The Infinite Way or the first class work in Africa and Australia. Few can realize the extent to which these trips were adventures, for few have carried a message of newly revealed principles to far away countries without advertising and "without purse or scrip."

The presentation of the message given me after I returned home from Holland was begun with the *Maui Advanced Work*, the *Hawaiian Village Open Work*, and the *Hawaiian Village Closed Class*. During the *Hawaiian Village Closed Class*, our students from Australia, New Zealand, England, Canada, the Mainland, and Hawaii experienced an atmosphere they will hardly be likely to forget and which, because of their own uplifted consciousness, they should be able to impart to those at home. This message, which will deepen and clarify itself with each additional class, should be studied, pondered, and practiced in accordance with the instructions given in the June, July, and August *Letters*, as well as with such additional instructions as we receive for the balance of the year.

After the work during August in San Diego, California, and Victoria and Vancouver, Canada, all of September will be spent in England where the heaviest schedule of lectures and class work we have ever had in England has been arranged. October takes us to our students in Holland. While there, I shall participate in an international conference on world peace, the membership of which is limited to those who have previously participated as speakers. Following that, there will be class work in Lausanne, Switzerland, for our Geneva and Lausanne students. The year's work will culminate in November with an intensive program of lecture and class work in New York and with the introduction of *The Art of Spiritual Healing* published by Harper and Brothers, and then, lectures in Chicago, and homeward bound for the holidays.

In Germany, a German translation of *The Art of Meditation* will be published this fall, and a German translation of *Practicing the Presence* is now in the process of being made. Furthermore, during October, arrangements will be concluded for the publication of the monthly *Letter* in German. The new British edition of *God, the Substance of All Form* should now be available, and *Metaphysical Notes*, which is to be published under the new title, *Conscious Union with God*, will soon go to press.

The principles which are now being so clearly imparted to you and which are to be embodied in your treatment and meditation work will bring you fruitage in proportion to your conscious practice of them. On April 8, 1959, an unfoldment was given me of which our entire student-body will become aware in varying measure, bringing new experiences of a spiritual nature and with "signs following." Ponder well the passage on the frontispiece of all Infinite Way writings for further illumination.

FREEING OURSELVES FROM UNIVERSAL CLAIMS

IN spiritual healing, there is always the temptation to try to improve the human scene. The first and normal reaction is to attempt to make a sick person well, to obtain employment for the unemployed, to bring supply to the needy, and happiness to the unhappy. Such persistent attempts at human betterment, however, usually result only in failure.

Even though you perceive the significance of this point at this moment, you probably will find it difficult in giving a treatment to refrain from the temptation to desire to change the appearance into an opposite, better appearance. The desire to improve human conditions is natural to you and to me, and it was undoubtedly natural also to Jesus Christ, or he would not have had to go away forty days to renew himself, nor would he have had to leave his disciples every once in a while for that same purpose, because the only renewal any of us ever needs is to break the mesmerism of appearances. That is the only reason we ever have to pray and commune with the Father; that is the only reason we ever have to go away to be still. There is no other reason.

Furthermore, even though many of us are not mesmerized by most forms of error, some of us are still mesmerized in a large measure by good humanhood. The destructive and evil aspects of human-hood rarely tempt us now, but many of us are still tempted by its seemingly more desirable aspects, which in the final analysis are but the opposite of the evil humanhood and in the end can be just as destructive.

Give Up All Attempts to Change the Human Picture

So it is that, when we sit down to help others, one of our first realizations must be, "I am not trying to change sick matter into healthy matter; I am not trying to change a little matter into a lot of matter; I am not trying to make unhappy people happy. My aim in this meditation is to realize, behold, and demonstrate the Christ." In other words, our function is to demonstrate Christhood—the Christ-hood of your being and mine. When we rise to that state of consciousness, we shall never try to get something or to get rid of something, to draw something to us or force something away from us. Our entire ministry will be a realization of the Christ.

In his true identity, every person is the Christ, the offspring of God; and there is nothing that you or I can do to change this one iota, and nothing we can do to make it so. It already is true. God already is the life of individual being; God already is the soul and the spirit and the mind; God already is the integrity of every individual. That was established in the beginning before Abraham was, but it is not manifest—it is not visible—until there is one individual who can sit in the silence and realize the Christ, which is the true spiritual identity of individual being.

In Christian mysticism, the word "Christ" is understood to mean that which we in our true identity are. Actually, it would make no difference if we were to speak of revealing the Buddha-nature of us, because that means exactly the same thing—the enlightened one, or Christ-self. The terminology is unimportant.

The Christ is not visible to the eyes, nor is It audible to the ears; the Christ cannot be touched with the fingers, nor smelled or tasted: The Christ is really a state of divine consciousness which you and I are. It is an incorporeality. In our true state of being, that is what we really are although that is not what we appear to be to one another. Looking out through the eyes, we behold a finite, limited, and material concept of that which actually is.

The field of art illustrates this point. To the person without a developed artistic sense, masterpieces of painting mean nothing more to him than so much colored paint on canvas, because he does not have an understanding of painting. In the same way, a person who has no appreciation of music might have the most glorious symphony or opera ever composed played for him and yet beg somebody to turn it off or stop the music because the sound offends his ears.

So it is in the area of spiritual living and spiritual healing. With our limited finite sense, we look out upon God's masterpiece—individual being. You and I are God's masterpiece, His own offspring, His own Self made individually manifest; but, beholding that masterpiece without spiritual apprehension, we judge it to be worthless. If you have spiritual perception, it makes no difference who calls upon you for help, whether it is someone mired in the deepest of sin or someone bound by a physical distortion beyond description. Notice the difference in the picture you behold when you sit with eyes closed to all appearances in this realization:

Father, I am not trying to change this picture; I am not trying to change the condition or the person. Awaken me out of this mesmeric dream, so that I do not judge by appearances, but see this person as he is, and I shall be satisfied with that likeness, because here is the Christ, the spiritual offspring of God.

Grant me Thy grace that I may see him as he is in his Divinity and behold this situation as it is. Reveal to me the Christ in this very place where there seems to be a human being.

As you sit in that silence, waiting, the Spirit of God touches, illumines, and inspires you; and for a brief, fleeting second, it is almost as if you could see or touch Reality. Sometimes in this deep moment of realization, the whole room is filled with the perfume of flowers, although there may not be a flower within miles of you. This sense of Reality may come as music, music that has no earthly sounds; it may come as a light or as a deep breath. What difference how it comes! What is coming to you is the very Spirit of God.

Whatever the way, if it is clear to you that you are not seeking to change a human being from bad to good, poor to rich, unemployed to employed, or sick to well, but that what you are seeking to behold is Divinity and not humanhood, then sooner or later, the great experience will come to you. It may only be for a moment, but in that momentary flash, your patient will be improved, benefited, healed, employed, or enriched—whatever the situation may demand.

The Object of Healing Is the Transformation of Consciousness

Certainly there are cases in which the fullness of the healing does not appear in that first moment of realization, no matter how deep it may be, and you may be called upon to repeat the process twice, ten, or a hundred times, because the opacity may lie with your patient or student in whom there must be a change of consciousness before harmony can be outwardly pictured.

One of the great stumbling blocks to healing is that the majority of people seeking help have too definite an idea of what it is they want, and of course their human desires may not fit in at all with the spiritual picture. Many of you know of my own struggle to increase my business during the early years of my study, of how I engaged no less than five different practitioners for that purpose, one after the other; and yet despite all this help and the dedicated work of each practitioner, my business grew worse and worse, until finally there was no business at all. That surely appeared to be a lack of demonstration, but actually it was a perfect demonstration. Had my business prospered, my going into this work might have been delayed or even completely prevented in this lifetime.

Many people come to us for help, but often they have a preconceived idea of what it is they want.

They have a predetermined idea of *how* harmony is to appear in their experience, and often even *when* it is to appear. Instead of responding to God's will, they resist God by deciding in their own minds how the demonstration should unfold, when, and to what extent. Satisfying the wants and desires of covetous human beings is not really a part of our ministry. Our ministry is the changing of a person's consciousness from a material sense of life to the spiritual awareness of life, from a material sense of religion to a spiritual sense of religion, and from a material sense of supply to a spiritual sense of supply.

Always remember that we are not healers of the body; we do not attempt to change the body at all. Our work changes the consciousness of an individual, and that changed consciousness appears outwardly as harmony, health, supply, companionship, or whatever the need may be.

Over and over the temptation will come, "I must save this person's life"; "I must restore this person's sanity"; or, "I must bring peace to this household." Resist such temptations to outline, because you have no way of knowing what the demonstration is to be. For example, peace may be the worst thing to have in a household for the spiritual progress of its members. Do not desire anything, and do not judge, criticize, or condemn anyone. Turn completely from the human scene with its appearances of good and evil and pray for the revelation of the Christ in human consciousness, for the revelation of spiritual identity, for the revelation of God's spiritual plan, or for spiritual illumination.

When we turn within, let us realize that we are turning within in order to behold the spiritual reality in place of the humanhood which is confronting us. When we have that second of spiritual realization which is interpreted by us to mean that we have beheld the very Christ of God, the very spiritual reality of being, this, then, touches the consciousness of the patient or student and begins to transform it.

All experience is transformed by the renewing of the mind. In other words, there is a gradual change from the man of earth to the man who has his being in Christ. A human being is the man of earth, but in his spiritual identity, he is that man who has his being in Christ. The goal of life is to "die daily" to the man of earth, which we are as human beings, so that there may be a conscious rebirth of spiritual being which is man's true identity.

Removing the Burden

In the very earliest books of The Infinite Way it has been made clear that, in our human ignorance, we are not responsible for the error that is touching our life, not even responsible for the sin, lack, hate, envy, or jealousy which may be the dominating motif. All of that is part of a universal activity which Paul called the carnal mind and which centuries later was referred to as "mortal mind." In The Infinite Way, the terms "universal belief," "universal hypnotism," and "universal mesmerism" are used to describe this vast universal ignorance which is the sum and substance of all the sin, disease, lack, limitation, and old age which hold the world in bondage. This universal or carnal mind of man is pumping its thought, beliefs, and theories into you and into me night and day, year in and year out.

Every carnal or material thought, whether of a physical, mental, moral, or financial nature, every thought of false ambition, greed, lust, hate, injustice, or unkindness is all part of this vast mental illusion, and every human being is subject to it. Each person becomes subject to some particular phase of it at whatever happens to be his most vulnerable spot.

All of this is brought about unconsciously, that is, without conscious thought on our part, and in most cases unconsciously on the part of anyone else. There is not a devil doing this to us in a personalized sense of devil, nor is there anybody wicked enough to be capable of doing it to humanity. It is an aggregation of the sum total of everything of a selfish or personal nature that has happened since the days of Adam, formed out of the original belief in two powers, good and evil. This sum total of evil is now floating about in this very room in which you are sitting. Some of it is in the room by virtue of nearby radios or television sets that may be carrying it. You are not aware of it because these sets are not plugged in or turned on, but nevertheless it is here; it is going through this room, and under its influence, you are responding to current medical and theological beliefs.

I have never yet met a person who could rightly be termed a sinner, if judged from the standpoint of whether or not he really and truly wanted to sin. Every sinner I have ever met has admitted sooner or later that he does not want any part of it, but that he does not know how to free himself of it, just as a person suffering from poverty might feel, "Certainly, I do not want any part of this. This is not part of me, or of my will or desire."

Then, where does it come from? It is being whispered into your subconscious below the level of conscious perception. You know nothing about it, but nevertheless you respond to it. It comes out of that same area of consciousness that may be likened to the activity of subliminal perception.[1]

As far back as the early 1930's, I began to see that evil is never personal and that it can be separated from any individual once he, himself, has realized that the time has come to be free of this suggestion. When anyone comes to us for help, he can be set free the moment we recognize, "This is not your fault; this is not your doing; you are not responsible for this: This is the carnal mind, a nothingness." Such a recognition makes it impossible for us to hold our patients or students in any form of condemnation, criticism, or judgment, and enables us to free most of those who come to us. It lifts such a load from our patients or students that their shoulders are thrust back quickly, and, although they may not know why, they feel a sense of freedom. The burden of guilt and responsibility has been lifted from their shoulders by realizing, "Why, this is not you. This is not a part of you: This is the carnal mind."

[1] For a further explanation of this subject, see the author's *The 1958 Infinite Way Letters* (London, England: L. N. Fowler & Co., Ltd., 1958). Pp. 200-218.

The Carnal Mind Is Not a Power

There is a second step to be taken: Since God is, and since God is infinity, immortality, eternality, and omnipotence, the carnal mind is not power. It has no power to express itself through us once we have realized God as the only power. It can only operate in the consciousness of a person who believes in two powers—whether or not he accepts these two powers consciously or unconsciously—and it operates until he consciously renounces the power of evil and recognizes it as non-power.

But the very moment a person realizes that the carnal mind with its sum total of evil, sin, disease, death, lack, limitation, and age is not power—is only an illusory belief in the universal mind, not in your mind or mine, but in the universal mind, and is therefore not a power—the evil is dissolved. Actually it had as much validity as has the statement that two times two equals five. Two times two is five is a tremendous power in the mind of the person who believes it because he will always be giving out five for four. But once it is recognized that two times two equals five is not an entity or an identity or a substance or a law, but a nothingness, we are free, and our patient is free.

At this stage of our spiritual unfoldment, if the carnal mind, or somebody operating in the area of subliminal perception, were to tell us to act in a certain way, we would not do it if it were contrary to our sense of right. We already know enough of the one mind so that we would not respond easily or quickly to that suggestion. When a higher state or stage of consciousness is reached, there are many more areas in which this universal carnal mind cannot find outlet through us because we have arrived at the point where we cannot be tempted by many of the things which tempt the majority of people. Usually we cannot even be tempted to fear, whether it be a war, bombs, or the next bit of infection or contagion about which we read in the newspapers.

In other words, the carnal mind has already lost a great deal of its power over us. If we were awakened in the morning and found ourselves completely without funds, I doubt that any of us would be unduly frightened because instantly the thought would come, "It makes no difference. God's manna falls every day, and God's grace is my sufficiency." And there would be no fear. But quite the reverse of this would happen to the person not knowing this and who therefore believed that lack was an actual condition.

Most of us are already at that stage where we very seldom, if ever, have a cold, grippe, the "flu," or any of those ailments that are common to people during inclement weather. It lies within our power to attain eighty or ninety percent of freedom from all the ills of this world by recognizing:

The carnal mind cannot find inlet or outlet through me, since in my true being, I am one with God; and because I am consciously one with God, all that the Father has is mine, and only that which is of the Father is mine. I am an instrument through which, and as which, God lives.

I am the inlet and the outlet for all that is heavenly and divine. There is no "me." That which the world identifies as "me" is God appearing as me, the life and allness of God made individually manifest. My oneness with God constitutes my oneness with that mind which was in Christ Jesus, my oneness with the very Soul which is God.

"The prince of this world cometh, and hath nothing in me."[1] The carnal mind may present itself to me, but I am not home to it; I do not receive or respond to it. I do not hear it, taste it, touch it, or smell it, for that which constitutes the carnal mind is not entity or identity, but illusory belief —an appearance. This picture of mortality which presents itself to me is a temptation to believe in the entity, identity, and reality of mortal creation.

I live by the grace of God which is my sufficiency, not by external things or persons. In the presence of God is fullness of life, and I no longer am dependent on people, thoughts, or things, since I am consciously one with my creative Principle, God, Spirit; and because of this realization, my life is spiritually governed and guided, spiritually fed and spiritually lived. It is the impartations from God which constitute my bread, wine, water, substance, my resurrection, and the harmony of my being.

A human being is only a human being because the carnal mind is accepted as a power, but we can "die daily" to our humanhood if in the morning and certainly at night before sleeping we make it a point of realization:

The so-called theories, opinions, and beliefs which constitute the whole of the carnal mind are not power: They have no avenue of expression and they have no law to sustain or maintain them.

I am one with God, and the qualities of God constitute my qualities. I am an instrument and an avenue through

[1] John 14:30.

199

which, and as which, God appears on earth. The intelligence of God, the love, the wisdom, and the grace of God find expression in me, through me, and as me to all of this world, for I and the Father are one.

Such conscious knowing of the truth spells the death of humanhood because the carnal mind is not whispering suggestions into our deadened mind and making us respond to them. The mystery of life is really not a mystery. The mystery of life harmonious is the understanding of our true nature and true identity and a conscious and constant relating of ourselves to our Source, and then realizing that over and beyond this, nothing is power, nothing is law, nothing is cause, and nothing can have effect.

When we experience a healing by turning to a practitioner for help, it is because the practitioner has nullified the carnal mind and its activity for us by knowing its non-power. It is true that some practitioners may know that that is what happens when a healing is witnessed, but many do not know how this principle operates. When we have need of a practitioner's help, it is only because this carnal mind has found expression in and through us. The remedy lies in nullifying it, and that can only be brought about through the realization, first, of its impersonal nature and then, secondly, of its non-power. We must impersonalize every form of error whenever we see it, hear it, taste it, touch it, or smell it—whether it concerns us, our patients, our students, or the strangers on the street. We nullify it, recognize its non-power, and impersonalize it. We impersonalize every phase of error, no matter what form it assumes.

Has not history proved that the assassination of kings and queens and emperors has never stopped tyranny? It never does and it never can, because the evil is not personal. As rapidly as one person is eliminated, we come face to face with the same evil in the next person. But the realization that evil is always impersonal could do much to free the world from all the dictators of the world.

We can bless the world by refusing to personalize error—by realizing that evil is not man-made, man-created, or man-perpetuated, but that all this carnality is the impersonal, universal mind of man, the personalized sense of mind—and then take that second step of realizing, "Yes, but since God is omnipotent, the carnal mind is not power. It is not presence or substance and has no activity and no law." Through such activity in our consciousness, the way may be opened and the mind may be sufficiently cleared of false beliefs for the divine idea of oneness, or unity, to break through, and eventually someone may come forth with a workable idea.

As we practice this in our daily experience, we shall find that less and less will we be responding to what Jesus called "this world." With the exception of those three specific temptations in the wilderness, Jesus overcame the temptations of this world, not by overcoming one temptation after another, but by recognizing, "Ye are of your father the devil."[1] In other words, he impersonalized them and then realized that they had no power—"Thou couldest have no power at all against me, except it were given

[1] John 8:44.

thee from above"[1]—there is no power save that which comes from God.

We are now at the point where we must take the position of advanced spiritual students who recognize the impersonal nature of evil, whether in high places or not, and hold to it, standing firmly on our understanding of the great fact that all evil is not only impersonal, but that it is not power. Evil has no avenue of operation, no vehicle of operation, and no law for its maintenance or sustenance.

TRAVELOGUE

This is a beautiful Sunday in Victoria, Canada, one of the few remaining urban places in the world where Sunday can be really peaceful and restful. Although "tomorrow" is already beginning to reach Victoria, there is still much of "yesterday" to be found here on Vancouver Island where the old world grace and charm of a typical English countryside invite relaxation and contemplation.

After the *Hawaiian Village Closed Class* in Honolulu, we flew to the West Coast July 29, stopping in San Francisco and Los Angeles en route to San Diego. Our primary object in going to San Diego was to become acquainted with a newborn grandchild, a dear little girl who is far noisier than her grandmother. But always, carrying the message of The Infinite Way takes precedence over personal or family considerations and is the dominant note in all our travels. So it was in San Diego.

Once again I was invited to speak for the Church of Religious Science, and the four talks given dealt

[1] John 19:11.

for the most part with meditation and the practice of the Presence and how these lead to the attainment of a life by Grace. For me, these meetings were a source of tremendous inspiration.

Upon learning that I was to be in San Diego for a few days, a small group of students asked for a closed class. To my surprise, instead of the less than two dozen who had requested the class, seventy-eight Infinite Way students appeared. How so many came from such far places without even notice of a class or without even the guarantee of a room in which to meet is one of the mysteries of the workings of God.

At this particular time, a labor conference of some 2,000 union men and their families filled the hotels and made accommodations scarce and a class-room practically impossible. Nevertheless, these seventy-eight determined students found places "prepared for them," and arrangements were made for morning sessions for this four-day class. El Cortez Hotel provided a different room each morning but always managed to have chairs and a table set up by ten o'clock for what was probably the most informal Infinite Way class ever held. I am sure that none of us will ever forget the experience—a class that came together spontaneously without formal arrangement, without notice, with no actual assurance that students would find accommodations, and certainly with no knowledge of where such a class could be held under the existing circumstances.

In the early years of The Infinite Way, there were many such spontaneously formed classes: in Desert Hot Springs and in San Francisco, California; in

Seattle, Washington; and once in Chicago. Always these have been productive of inspiring experiences, and so I am sure that rich fruitage will come from this San Diego class.

By the time this reaches you, we shall be getting ready for Holland, Germany, and Switzerland, and the return to New York by November 1. Now we have a few delightful days ahead of us with students in Victoria and Vancouver, and then a stopover in San Francisco to meet the jet that carries us to London.

PRAYER AND TREATMENT
THROUGH THE SPIRIT

PROBABLY one of the greatest differences between
the message of The Infinite Way and most other
religious teachings, whether orthodox or metaphysical, is that in The Infinite Way no power is
given to any word that is spoken or thought. No
confidence is placed in mere statements of truth,
wordy prayers, affirmations, or denials, unless these
are uttered out of a realized spiritual consciousness.

No treatment or prayer can rise any higher than
the consciousness from which it emanates. None of
the truth read in books and none of the statements
of truth made to a person—none of this is spiritual
power unless it flows out of an attained spiritual
consciousness, that is, unless the person making the
statement is in the Spirit when he voices truth,
writes, thinks, declares it, or prays. Unless he is in
the Spirit, his prayer or his treatment will rise no
higher than the level of his own mind.

If you pray or treat with your three-dimensional
human consciousness, some measure of human
demonstration or human improvement can be
expected, but the amount of that fruitage will only
be in proportion to your human faith, or belief, or
to your powers of mental concentration. It is somewhat like the fifteen people who are healed every

year out of the hundred thousand or so who make pilgrimages to Lourdes. Those fifteen people are healed because of the intensity of their own faith and emotion, and their healing has nothing to do with God.

Much metaphysical healing work is accomplished by the faith and emotion of the practitioner, as well as by that of the patient. Sometimes patients bring with them a great deal of hope and confidence when they turn to a practitioner for help—hope, faith, and confidence in God, in the practitioner, or sometimes in a particular approach to truth.

But real spiritual demonstration—actual spiritual healing—is largely dependent upon the ability of the individual who is the practitioner to rise, first of all, into an atmosphere of Spirit, and then in this consciousness of God's presence, any word uttered, any idea thought, or any statement made or written is power. In such a state of consciousness, whatever comes through is God-power, expressing Itself through the individual who is at that moment acting as a practitioner.

It is for this reason that it is foolish for an Infinite Way student to attempt to give a treatment or even acknowledge a letter from someone asking for help, until he is convinced that he is in the Spirit. It is a form of egotism to believe that you or I have the power to benefit anyone of ourselves, or by our understanding of what is in books. Even if we could memorize everything that is in every one of The Infinite Way writings and in addition to that all the scriptures of the world, it would be valueless.

If, however, we rise in spiritual awareness to where we attain a measure of realization of God's presence, then it is really unimportant what words are spoken or written to a student or patient, or even what is thought, because the presence of God has been realized and It is doing Its work. Your response to a call for help may be a simple, "I will help you"; "I am with you"; or on the other hand you may write twelve pages of metaphysics. It makes no difference what form your response takes, because if you are in the Spirit, the work will be done.

Even though I am always, in a measure, living in the Spirit because of my constant meditation, I never attempt to answer my mail until I feel the flow of the Spirit within me; and then I rarely answer more than one, two, or three letters before I stop for further meditation. Furthermore, every time I come to a letter that does not bring an immediate response in my consciousness, I immediately stop and meditate, because any letter that I might write has no more power than a letter that anyone else might write, if it comes out of my mind. But if I am in the Spirit, then Its power flows; and, so far as healing is concerned, it would make no difference if I did not write any letter at all. Writing the letter is only a concession to patients and students who might possibly think that their letter had not been received or had not been given attention if no reply were forthcoming.

Actually, when I am in the Spirit, however, the healing work is done when the call for help registers itself in my consciousness. I do not have to receive the message in my mind. In other words, it makes no difference whether a letter is delivered to me or lost in the mail, whether a cable reaches me or not. The registering in my consciousness takes place when a person is impelled to make contact with me. Whether that urge takes the form of attempting to reach me by telephone, cable, or letter, if I am in the Spirit, I will receive the call at that moment, even if I never receive the letter, cable, or telephone call. However, because very few students or patients are prepared to accept that height of unfoldment, every cable, telephone call, or letter is always answered and answered promptly.

Do not expect anything of any treatment or prayer you may give, or at least do not expect too much of it, unless you have first brought yourself into the atmosphere of God so that you feel a certain warmth within yourself, a gentleness, a Presence, something that assures you that you are in the presence of God. Then you may be certain that regardless of what form your message takes, or your treatment or prayer, it will be effective. At that stage, then, it matters not whether your prayer is intercessory, whether it is a petition, an affirmation, a denial, or a complete silence, because it is not any *form* of prayer or treatment, but the actual Presence, that does the work.

Recognize the Divine Source

Each of us is inwardly connected with an infinite storehouse, just as every tree and bush in the valley at Halekou Place is connected with the same soil, and through that soil, with the same inner life that permeates the soil. Everything in the valleys and mountains there is connected with the same infinite Source, but if there is a barrier between the roots and the free flow of that one life through the soil, then there will be dead trees or dead plants.

Our relationship to the one Life is much the same as that of an individual tree to the earth. Each one of us is an individual, the visible expression of an invisible Life. When we know this and consciously make contact with It, we no longer have a life of our own: It is Its life that flows out into expression as our experience; and our Source being infinite, our demonstration is as infinite as we are able to accept.

Although the world in reality is one with its infinite Source, it is not consciously so. The entire secret of life is bound up in the one word "consciousness." If I am consciously aware of this infinite Fountain, Source, or Storehouse, and if I consciously draw upon It by realizing my oneness with It and letting the flow take place, then my life is lived in, by, through, and as Spirit.

But if I think that my life is dependent upon my efforts, my physical strength or mental power, my education or my understanding, then I am limiting myself to my human endowments. The very moment, however, that I begin to acknowledge that He that is within me is greater than he that is in the world, the minute I begin to acknowledge that He performeth that which is given me to do, the minute I acknowledge that there is a He, in other words that there is an infinite Source, whether we call it He, She, or It—the moment I acknowledge that my life is the product of Something greater than my human selfhood, then I set about making contact with It. That acknowledgment, however, is only the first step. If that itself were all there is to it, then many more would be enjoying spiritual fruitage than are at present experiencing it, but there is another and far more important step—that second step of actual contact which must be taken.

The message of The Infinite Way is divided into two parts. The first part is found in the statement, "I and my Father are one,"[1] and therefore, all that the Father has is mine. This means that our only existence is as an outlet for an infinite Storehouse which is invisible, and that it is possible for us to be consciously one with this infinite Storehouse, this fountain of Good.

The second part of the message of The Infinite Way deals with how to attain conscious union with that infinite Storehouse. Through studying the correct letter of truth, seeing it with the eyes and hearing it with the ears, meditating upon the Word, cogitating, contemplating, abiding in the Word and letting it abide in us, and specifically knowing the truth in our treatment work, eventually there comes that inner stillness in which we no longer declare the word—no longer pray, treat, or affirm—but are brought to a state of silence in which we can be receptive and feel Its flow. That is the ultimate of the Message.

[1] John 10:30.

Attaining Inner Stillness

When you come to that point where you consciously remind yourself in a thousand different ways that all that the Father *is*, is flowing into expression as your individual being, one day you arrive at the place where you really believe it and have the conviction of it. In that conviction, you rest from statements and thoughts in a complete stillness with your ears open. Sooner or later, every serious student who perseveres in his conscious knowing of the truth arrives at that place where there will come a moment of complete stillness. That moment may be of only a second's duration, but it is an absolute silence in which, just for a second, even the mind is still. As this practice is continued, it becomes easier to attain that moment of silence, and those moments of silence gradually prolong themselves into two seconds, ten seconds, and thirty seconds.

With continued practice, it eventually becomes possible to settle back into that stillness almost at will at any given moment of the day or night. And yet, because the mesmerism of the world is so entrenched in consciousness, even with a developed state of consciousness, there may be times when it may take a whole hour of dwelling on the letter of truth before silence is attained.

That, however, does not necessarily mean an hour of sitting trying to force this silence. It may mean one, two, or three minutes of sitting, waiting, and then getting up and walking around before settling down to try it over again—or reading for a short period of time and then returning to it. Do not try to take heaven by storm. If peace does not come in a few minutes, get up and do something else—eat or drink something, read, walk up and down the room, or take a walk outside, and then return to your meditation. Sometimes it is even wise to lie down and take a nap.

Eventually, the awareness of the Spirit comes, growing in intensity until the day comes when it remains with you in a measure all the time. Regardless of what you may be doing in the outer world, there is always a little area of consciousness which is unmoved by the human scene. When the Spirit of God is upon you, that is, when you are completely relaxed and feel the Presence, anything you do or think is with spiritual power, and it is then that you will understand the real meaning of the word "faith."

If the tens of millions of prayers that are uttered every day flowed out from the Spirit, they would be productive of a complete change of consciousness on earth. But because they are uttered from the mind, even those who voice them usually are not too hopeful of receiving an answer. I am sure that most people who pray would be shocked if they awakened the next day and found a whole new consciousness, but that is only because the human mind cannot really grasp the idea of faith.

Faith is of such a nature that wherever it is, fruition is. Faith is something more than blind hope, something more than an anticipation of good. Faith is an actual contact with God, and where there is no actual contact with God, there is no faith: There is only a human hope, and it is a hope without reason. Real faith exists only where there is spiritual contact.

Faith is a power, and since that is true, you can readily understand that faith is not something you, yourself, generate. Faith is something that takes possession of you. Faith is the Spirit of God, Itself, the gift of God. It is a quality that transcends anything that the human mind can grasp or understand. Therefore, it is not our concern to develop a faith or declare that we have faith. Our one major concern should be to be silent until the Spirit of God takes over and is felt.

Regardless of what truths you know when you sit down to meditate, to treat, or to heal, always be sure that you do not consider that your work is complete —your treatment or your prayer—until in one way or another you have received the assurance of God's presence. Then, eventually, you will see why it is that you can no longer have faith in anything in the world of effect as spiritual power. You will know that that spiritual power is only present when the Spirit of God is present. The Master said, "The Spirit of the Lord is upon me, because he hath anointed me to preach the gospel to the poor; he hath sent me to heal the brokenhearted, to preach deliverance to the captives, and recovering of sight to the blind, to set at liberty them that are bruised."[1] He would never have said that he could do these things unless the Spirit of the Lord were upon him, for no one knew better than he that of himself he could do nothing.

[1] Luke 4:18.

Consciousness is the secret. By observation, you will soon learn that everything within range of your consciousness is taking on the quality of your consciousness. The trees and flowers in your garden or the crops in your fields respond not only to the amount of rain or fertilizer nature provides, but they take on an additional richness when they are embraced in your consciousness. You will also find that the people who are embraced in your consciousness, whether your family, patients, or students, experience a greater degree of harmony in their affairs because of being a part of that consciousness.

The Twelve, the Seventy, and the Two Hundred became something more than ordinary human beings because they were a part of the Master's consciousness. They were able to go out into the world, and by virtue of his consciousness, they partook of that consciousness, and then when they went out those who became part of *their* consciousness in turn partook of their illumined state of consciousness. That is what is meant by the phrase, "in his name."

Wherever the disciples and apostles moved, miracles took place—in prison and out, in lions' dens and out—because they were all included in that Christ-consciousness of which Jesus was so fully aware and which operated through the disciples and apostles for the benefit of others. Those others who came within range of their consciousness began to manifest greater harmonies, and then, in turn, some of those who were not satisfied merely with demonstrations of harmony began seeking the attainment of that Christ-consciousness themselves.

The first fruitage apparent to a person after contact with a spiritually illumined person has been established is that greater harmonies begin to come into his experience. But that is only a primary stage after which the individual himself must come into an actual awareness of this Presence.

One person living in the consciousness of God's presence can bring tremendous harmony into the lives of everyone who touches his or her consciousness, but that is only a first step. That is why the Master said, "If I go not away, the Comforter will not come unto you."[1] I have seen some beautiful healings come into the lives of people—dramatic changes from lack to abundance, from disease to health, from a disturbed state of mind to peace, or from discord and inharmony to harmony. Unfortunately, I have also witnessed how many of the people who have experienced these healings have not retained that which they had gained because they themselves did not make the effort to attain that same consciousness which wrought these mighty works.

The Christ-consciousness is not easily attained, and that is why students give up so readily. The way is straight and narrow, and few there be who attain it. It demands a high price—the highest price—humility; and that quality, no human being has in too large an amount. But nothing less than complete humility brings that consciousness. True

[1] John 16:7.

humility is not just a pious looking face; it is far more than that. It is the ultimate and actual acknowledgment that one's human identity is nothing, and this produces that complete vacuum into which, and through which, the Spirit of God can operate. That is not achieved quickly, and even when it has been achieved, it can easily be lost. Spiritual consciousness has to be nurtured, it has to be fed, and always in its unfoldment, humility is the greatest factor of all.

The Fruitage of an Attained State of God-Consciousness

The passage on spiritual illumination found on the frontispiece of all Infinite Way books means that we are united with one another, if so be we consciously maintain our oneness with God. The theme of *Metaphysical Notes*,[1] "My conscious oneness with God constitutes my oneness with all individual spiritual being and idea," is literally true. When this Spirit of God is upon us, we are not only one with God, but we are one with all spiritual creation— human, animal, vegetable, and mineral. We are one with those who are attuned to us, and whatever degree of upliftment we are, or have, they experience. That is why students throughout this world are receiving some benefit from my attained state of spiritual consciousness, but that is only so that the nature of that contact and what it can do may be revealed to them, to the end that they also will strive to attain this inner conscious contact.

[1] This book by the author is now published in a revised edition under the title, *Conscious Union with God* (London, England: L. N. Fowler & Co., 1960).

The first indication that you have attained conscious contact with the Father within is not merely the measure of harmony that comes to you, but probably more significant than that are the harmonies that you are able to bring to others. You may still think that there is far too little harmony in your life, but surely none of us should ever want to be rid of a problem until the problem is replaced by a consciousness of perfection. There is little point in being physically healthy, if you are in a state of consciousness which will make it possible for you to become sick again tomorrow. There is no use in amassing a huge amount of dollars, if you are still in the state of consciousness where you can be in lack tomorrow. So the most important step is the attainment of the consciousness of good, and then the health, the supply, the companionship, or whatever it may be unfolds as an aftermath.

The attempt to attain health, supply, companionship, or whatnot will continue to be a barrier to your spiritual demonstration; whereas, releasing yourself from the desire for the attainment of any condition of life so that you can give yourself wholeheartedly to attaining the consciousness of the Presence will eventually result in your attaining a conscious contact with your Source. From then on, you will have no demonstration to make because whatever is required flows day by day as it is needed, and often with twelve baskets full left over.

The demonstration of things and conditions is not our work: Our work is attaining that inner awareness, that inner stillness and peace, and then letting it perform its work.

Do not expect fruitage in the outer experience except in proportion to the attainment of this inner peace, and even if you have greater demonstrations than you would have believed possible, do not be too happy about them, because they are only a natural consequence of an inner attainment. Enjoy the things of the outer world—that is what they are for. The Master would never have taught that you are entitled to fulfillment and that it is the Father's good pleasure to give you every good thing in this world, if he had not meant that you should enjoy them, but never become involved with things as such. Always remember that the source of all joy and satisfaction is the attainment of the Spirit, and then you will not be trapped into thinking that things of themselves are something.

Never separate yourself from your good by believing that the harmonies that come into your experience, or the experience of those around you, are other than the fruitage of *your* attained state of consciousness. Do not make the mistake of believing that Jesus Christ is a born Son of God, and therefore separate and apart from all other men, nor the metaphysical mistake of separating Jesus from the Christ, saying, "Oh, Jesus did not do that miracle— the Christ did." Never separate Jesus from the Christ, because without Jesus, there would have been no Christ visible on earth at that time.

Many practitioners have ultimately lost their way by making statements such as, "I had nothing to do with this healing—God did it." That immediately separates them from God. As a matter of fact, there is no such God as the God they are talking about, because the only God operating is their own attained and realized state of God-consciousness.

So with you. When you are the instrument for a healing, for you to try to separate that healing from the activity of your consciousness is to set up a God separate and apart from you. If your patients had not found you, where would they have been? Could they have found a God separate and apart from you? No, there was no God standing around on the street corner, and there was not a God sitting in their home. They found their harmony when they found you because you knew that *I* and the Father are consciously one; you knew that where you are, God is, and where God is, you are, for God and you are indivisible and inseparable.

If I should be the instrument through which a healing came to you and, when you expressed gratitude for the healing, if I should say to you, "Do not thank me. I did not do it," you might well reply, "Well, then, how is it that it did not happen before I found you?" You know the answer. Realized God-consciousness is the secret. Everybody is one with God, but despite that fact we cannot turn to anyone we meet on the street and receive healing through him. The reason that the person of realized God-consciousness is consciously one with God is not because he declares it, but because he first believed and accepted it as a correct statement and then set about attaining it.

You are one with God. Yes, of course you are, but that will not heal anybody. First, you must consciously accept that relationship and then you must set about attaining it. When you have felt that

Presence, you are so completely one with God that you cannot separate the Christ from yourself. When you are consciously one with God and have the awareness of that Presence, blessings flow.

Do not attempt to separate Jesus and the Christ. Acknowledge that the Christ and Jesus are one, and that all that the Christ is, Jesus is—because of oneness. Thou seest Jesus, thou seest the Father that sent him. That is a universal truth about every one of us in proportion to our attainment of the consciousness of it. "I and my Father are one.[1] . . . the Father that dwelleth in me, he doeth the works."[2]

Do not separate yourself from the Father by saying, "I had nothing to do with the healing." Of course you did. Many of you are devoting your whole life to doing the works of God; many of you are giving every conscious moment to that purpose; many of you are giving yourself—heart, soul, mind, and dollars—to it. How, then, can you honestly turn around and say, "I had nothing to do with it," when it is your whole life, your whole life's hope, ambition, and the object of attainment. Never make the mistake of separating yourself from God, but never believe that unless you are consciously present with God, you are anything other than a branch that is cut off. The branch separated from its source cannot expect spiritual fruitage.

When you are one with the Father and when you daily establish yourself in that relationship, then anything that you can expect of God can be expected of you. Even if it is raising the dead, it is possible to you —*in proportion to that oneness* with the Spirit. When the

[1] John 10:30.   [2] John 14:10.

220

Spirit of the Lord God is upon you, then are you ordained to bring harmony into this world by virtue of that contact and that oneness.

TRAVELOGUE

In a few days we shall have completed our work in England and will then fly to Munich, Germany, to meet our new publisher. From there, we fly to the Hague, Holland, for lectures and a closed class, after which I shall have two days with the International Conference which I addressed last year and whose meetings are not open to the public this year, but only to those who have previously addressed the Conference. This, of course, will make the occasion one of an entirely different nature than before, and out of it may come something new in the way of unfoldment, so of course I look forward to this experience with a great deal of joy.

Next on our itinerary is Geneva, Switzerland, where we shall be met and taken by automobile to Lausanne for nine or ten days, during which time there will be a closed class for the approximately fifteen students who have been studying the Writings and hearing the Recordings. This will be the first Infinite Way class in Switzerland, beginning modestly as have many of our classes in new countries with a small enrollment, but always these first classes have proved to be just the planting of the seed from which later rich fruitage has come.

To tell you that after the lectures and class in San Diego we went to Victoria and Vancouver, Canada, and found a continuing of that deep and rich consciousness which opened first in the Hawaiian

Village Closed Class, and to tell you that the work in London and the suburbs has been of a nature never before experienced in all our work in The Infinite Way, and that this continued in Manchester would be merely to tell you of effects— of larger lecture audiences and greater numbers of students in the closed classes. In the ordinary human sense of things, all these beautiful effects would, of course, be a cause for thanksgiving, especially in this month of November when so much attention is paid to the giving of thanks and to pondering those things for which we have reason to be thankful.

The events which have transpired in 1959, however, are only effects, but behind these effects is the one Cause, and were it not for that Cause, there would be no experiences in the world of effect for which to be thankful. But it is well to remember that as long as we dwell consciously in Cause, there will always be fruitful experiences.

When I was sent home from Holland last year to remain quiet and apart from public work, it was for the express purpose of receiving a message to carry out in 1959; but at that same time it was told me that even more things than the message would be given me, because in the forthcoming year the message was to become more universal and would no longer be confined to the metaphysical world.

A series of instructions came to me over a period of some months, which culminated in ten Hawaiian tapes, containing a message pin-pointing the specific and unique principles which constitute the heart and soul of the message of The Infinite Way. Along with these principles also came further instruction as to how these principles were to be applied in the developing of a spiritual healing consciousness.

On April 8, 1959, the revelation came that just as the Christ-consciousness had worked through me as my consciousness throughout these years of healing and teaching work and had performed the work given me to do, so this Christ-consciousness—*My* consciousness—would now become the consciousness of our students, more especially of our working students in all parts of the world. It was made clear that this *My* consciousness would now activate the message of The Infinite Way, not merely through Joel, but through all those who were engaged in any phase of Infinite Way work; and all the way from the Hawaiian Village Closed Class to the London and Manchester lectures and classes, the fruitage of the Christ-consciousness, of this *My* consciousness, is apparent. And so you will realize that gratitude must be deep, not only mine but yours, too, that *My* consciousness—the Christ-consciousness—is now the consciousness of the individuals who comprise the student body, as well as the working body, of The Infinite Way.

Many of you have done better healing work this year and have had healings beyond anything experienced before, and so my message to you is that you be not only grateful for your healings, for your bettered life, or for the influence which you may have been, but deeply grateful that *My* consciousness, the Christ-consciousness, is now yours, and therefore *My* peace has been given to you—not the peace the world gives, but a spiritual peace, a spiritual harmony and prosperity. It now remains only for you to abide in the consciousness of this truth in order to watch It as It multiplies Itself in your experience and then partake of Its fruitage.

Arrangements have been made whereby our English tapes can now be duplicated in England for the students of the British Dominions, thereby relieving the amount of work in the Tape Department in Hawaii and reducing the cost of these tapes to students in the Dominions. Arrangements have also been made for the publication of our writings and the monthly *Letter* in German and of course this, too, must be understood to be the fruitage of *My* consciousness, so there is cause for gratitude, not primarily that the books are to be published in German, and thereby another country of many millions of people opened to this message of spiritual truth, but rather that *My* consciousness, the Christ-consciousness, is operating also in Germany, bringing Its harmonies and Its grace to all those there who are receptive and responsive. Please remember that all of this is the fruitage of the Spirit, and it is the Spirit which we glorify.

Last week it was my joy and privilege to attend the annual meeting of the Lodge of Living Stones in Leeds, England, the only Masonic Lodge in the world authorized to teach esoteric Masonry, and to be given the glorious opportunity of acting as travelling ambassador. Therefore, from now on, I shall set aside one evening in every city and country to which I travel to meet with such Masons and their friends who may be interested in hearing further of this work. *The Meaning of Masonry* and *The Masonic*

Initiation, written by W. L. Wilmshurst, the founder of the Lodge of Living Stones, explain the esoteric Masonic principles which may be made practical in the daily life of Masons, just as The Infinite Way writings reveal to the world the esoteric principles of religion which, when practiced, bring into individual and collective experience spiritual harmonies, spiritual abundance, and the demonstration of life eternal.

You will all be happy to know that our schedule for 1960 is fast shaping up and that it will include lectures in Fresno and Sacramento, California; lectures and a closed class in Los Angeles; lectures in Portland, Oregon; lectures and a closed class in Seattle, Washington; talks in Denver, Colorado; Kansas City, Missouri; and Indianapolis, Indiana; with lectures and a closed class in Chicago. While arrangements have not yet been completed, it seems fairly certain that there will also be lectures in Toledo, Ohio; and Grand Rapids, Michigan, as well as lectures and closed class work in Washington, D.C. Arrangements have been made for a return trip to England in 1960 in order to carry on an even more extensive program of work than on this last trip and in time for me to give another address to the Masonic Lodge in Leeds, England.

Students, please join with me in secret, sacred, humble thanks that the Spirit of God is upon us, that Its glory fills us, and that Its life and law appear in our experience as God's grace.

CHRISTHOOD

RUNNING throughout the early history of the Hebrew people as recorded in the Bible is one central theme—the revelation of the Christ. All the prophets, major and minor, in some degree demonstrated the omnipresence of good in the midst of darkness, despair, lack, limitation, starvation, and danger. All the major Hebrew prophets protected their people from the disasters of war and the depredations of neighboring nations; protected them from famine, lack, and limitation; protected them from greater physical powers than their own; and overcame the handicaps that tended to prevent them from securing some measure of education and economic and political independence. In other words, they demonstrated the Christ.

Even though nowhere in any Hebrew literature with which I am familiar does it seem to be recognized that what every one of these prophets was demonstrating was in reality the activity and presence of the Christ in human consciousness; nevertheless, these great demonstrations of protection, supply, and harmony, as narrated in the books of the Old Testament, were not tricks of magic, making something appear out of nothing: They were demonstrations of the presence of the Christ under every adverse circumstance and condition.

The point is that not only is God power, but a person can demonstrate this power, and the individual demonstration of the power of God is tangible evidence of the activity of the Christ in human consciousness. God is one and God is power, and the individual showing forth of this God-power is the Christ made manifest, the Word made flesh. Only as we read the record of the various Hebrew prophets, do we catch a glimpse of the fact that they themselves realized the omnipresence of God-power in them and recognized that they individually were exemplifying It.

The New Testament is a continuation of the history of the Hebrew people, but of a people now raised to a higher dimension of life, and that by one of its rabbis, Jesus the Christ, who taught a new way of life which had not heretofore been revealed in Hebrew Scripture and which therefore required a whole new scripture, a testament to set forth his teaching of the higher revelation of God-power as individualized in human consciousness—a New Testament.

With this comes a second revelation: God is not a power over other powers; It is not a great something that is wielded over anyone; It does not war with neighboring nations. Now we begin to learn that these powers that the great Jehovah God has been battling are not power, but only something that will destroy the enemy powers and not something that will protect us from the enemy power. The New Testament reveals that there are no enemy powers.

In the New Testament, it is no longer merely the power of God that is recorded, but now the emphasis is on the power of God as shown forth through the man Jesus, through John, the beloved disciple, and later through Paul. We learn about a God that is one, but we also learn that this one God is within us, that Its kingdom—Its realm and Its reign—is within us.

Hebrew Scripture before the days of the Master did not reveal anything of that nature, although it did reveal a God who is one, one power, and here and there it referred to this God in the midst of us which is mighty. But the Hebraic teaching was not brought to a focus as God-power individualized, as is the Christ-teaching in the New Testament, where we find that the kingdom of God is within. There, God is brought down to individual sonship, to Christhood—the allness of the Father made manifest as the Son in individual consciousness. It is the same power, but now it is within us.

That brings us to the central theme of Christhood, which means God made individually manifest. Every demonstration of God-power is a revelation of the Christ because it is individual consciousness showing forth the activity, presence, and power of God. If this were not true, there would be a God sitting up high above us, and we would be sitting around waiting for this power to act upon us.

The activity of God is an activity that takes place within individual consciousness, and with such men as Abraham, Isaac, Jacob, Moses, Elijah, Isaiah, Jesus, John, and Paul showing forth this power for all their world to see, it became God-power individually demonstrated. That clarifies the meaning of the biblical statement that the Father and the Son are one. God is infinite universal being, and Christhood is the individual showing forth of Godhood. Without the demonstration of God in individual experience, so far as we are concerned, there is no God.

The Activity of Truth in Individual Consciousness Reveals the Christ

The activity of the Christ is possible to you and to me in the measure that we can grasp it and live it, but it is just as available to anybody in the world who is willing to devote time, effort, thought, money, and study to it. It does require all of those things. It requires devotion because Christ-consciousness is not merely the acquisition of knowledge: It is the development of a state of consciousness.

The truth we imbibe is only the foundation for the development of this consciousness. While it is possible to reduce this teaching to a dozen statements, more or less, and learn those dozen points, knowing them will not heal because while we may know all the principles, along with them, we also know seventy-five other things that we have picked up in our life which are not true, but which we still believe. A period of self-discipline and training is necessary to arrive at that place where not only do we know these principles, but we do not accept into our consciousness anything but these principles, and when that happens all our superstitious beliefs about physical and mental powers are left behind. To reach that state requires the development of consciousness, and while it is true that the whole power of God is made manifest as individual consciousness—as the Son—before that can be demonstrated, it has to be built into our consciousness.

This revelation of the Christ, the Son and the Father as one, has spread to peoples throughout the entire world, and as the Christ-doctrine has spread, it has embraced those in all lands and of all races, so that the world should have arrived at a point today where the revelation of the Christ is not confined to any denomination or sect, where it has no denominational or sectarian meaning whatsoever, but includes any person who has accepted the doctrine of the allness of God individually expressed.

What counts is the acceptance of spiritual power in individual consciousness, and such a consciousness is the Christ. And what is this spiritual power? A power over powers? No, it is an acknowledgment of only one power, and unless we acknowledge only one power, we shall be continually battling germs here, lack there, and floods some other place. The person imbued with Christ-consciousness, however, does not go up and down the world battling, but lets his light shine so that anyone who perceives this light in him can go to him and ask, "Give me some of this."

The Bible is a revelation of the Christ, a revelation of the infinite nature of God individually demonstrated, but requiring the activity of truth in individual consciousness to bring it forth. It is the realization that God is not sitting up in the sky and man waiting down here on earth for that God to bring peace on earth. Peace on earth comes as an activity of truth and love in consciousness, but it has to begin in the consciousness of an individual, spread from that individual to a group, spread from that group to a community, and so on around the world.

When people drop their sense of resistance to one another in the realization, not that all people are good and will not take advantage of one another, but in the realization of God as individual being; and when individuals on an ever widening scale begin to acknowledge God as the source of all being, the universal peace which has already been established in consciousness will become an externalized reality. As we begin to demonstrate that in a roomful of people, gradually the world will demonstrate it in a worldful.

The Demonstration of Christhood

The allness of God is made evident, tangible, and visible as individual being, but it is still the Father. "I and my Father are one.[1] . . . He that hath seen me hath seen the Father"[2] even though the Father is greater than I. The allness of the Father appears as the consciousness of the Son, and so the consciousness of the Son is as immortal and as eternal as that of the Father. Nowhere else can we find that principle revealed except in the doctrine of Christhood—the allness of the Father made manifest as the Son, the all-power of the Father made manifest as God giving the Son dominion. But God does not

[1] John 10:30.   [2] John 14:9.

really give the Son dominion: *God is dominion expressed as the Son*—the Father and Son, always one.

So we, as individual being, find our allness in God; and only as we find our health in God, as we find our wealth in God, our harmony of being in God, as God's harmony, God's health, God's wealth, do we find our own harmony, health, and wealth to be immortal, eternal, and infinite.

A demonstration of healing or supply is not a demonstration of health or a demonstration of money: It is a demonstration of Christhood—the activity of Christhood has been witnessed. When Moses brought forth a cloud by day and a pillar of fire by night, when he brought forth water from a rock, opened the Red Sea, or when manna fell from the sky, it was not a demonstration of supply or protection: It was a demonstration of Christhood.

Today, every time we are responsible for the healing of a cold, a headache, indigestion, cancer, or tuberculosis, please remember that it is a demonstration of Christhood: We have demonstrated Christhood as the identity of our patient or student; we have demonstrated the power and presence of God in individual consciousness, the kingdom of God on earth.

Every demonstration of the healing and redeeming power of God is evidence that the Father is the Son. The glory of the Father manifests as the immortality, health, harmony, wholeness, and completeness of the Son. This is the demonstration of Christhood.

*   *   *

A mystic, in the height of spiritual illumination, pierces the visible and beholds the invisible Presence or Power at work. His deeper vision enables him to see through every visible person and object and witness the activity of Spirit appearing as form. Every person who has attained conscious union with God has been granted glimpses of the Infinite Invisible which is producing the outer universe and renewing it continuously.

Something like that takes place in the experience of the practitioner of spiritual healing. At a certain point in his treatment or meditation, the activity of the mind ceases; and he achieves a momentary glimpse of the real man, that invisible portion of him called the Son of God, which is the Christ of individual being. Each one of us has an invisible Selfhood, of which the visible is but the outer form. This, you can prove for yourself by closing your eyes and realizing that you, yourself, are behind those eyes, but *you* are not visible. That which you see with your eyes is but your outer form or body, but the real "you" is behind those eyes. There is a "you," and that "you" is invisible, eternal, and immortal. That "you" is the very presence of God. It is for this reason that the place whereon you stand is holy ground, because wherever you are, there the very presence of God is, looking out at the world through your eyes.

With the intellect, I cannot perceive you, nor can I know you through the processes of the mind. Not even your own mother has ever really known you, nor has your husband or wife. There is a "you" which is unknown to anyone in this world but you, yourself, unknown to anyone except those spiritually illumined souls who have attained conscious union with God or those spiritually enlightened practitioners who have achieved a sufficient measure of illumination to perceive your spiritual Selfhood.

It is this vision which results in healing. When the practitioner glimpses, even momentarily, the Christ of you, that in you which transcends your physical and mental sense of being, then, in that instant of spiritual conception—immaculate conception—you are born of the Spirit. It is your practitioner who conceives you in your spiritual identity, and this true identity is later brought forth into visible manifestation as spiritual demonstration.

And the angel answered and said unto her, The Holy Ghost shall come upon thee, and the power of the Highest shall overshadow thee: therefore also that holy thing which shall be born of thee shall be called the Son of God.

Luke 1:35

That experience comes to every dedicated spiritual practitioner. When he is meditating, the Holy Ghost comes upon him, the power of the Highest overshadows him, and then, in that split-second of conception, the Christ is revealed—the Son of God is born in him.

Such an experience does not remove your ills and

234

give you good health: It removes your humanhood and restores you to your spiritual identity. Whereas the mental practitioner merely transforms a belief of sickness into a belief in health, the spiritual practitioner, that person who lives a life of conscious oneness with God, lives for only one purpose, and that purpose is that the Holy Ghost may descend and remain upon him and this power of the Highest overshadow him. In that overshadowing, spiritual conception takes place: The Christ is conceived, and then is It born in you; but It can be born only in the death of your humanhood and in the revelation and demonstration of your spiritual Self-hood.

The Descent of the Holy Ghost

This period of the descent of the Holy Ghost and the power of the Highest overshadowing you comes only after you have attained some measure of the realization of God as the one power and have given up all attempts to fight error or to use truth to overcome evil—when you have ceased struggling, knowing full well that the battle is not yours, but God's—"not by might, nor by power, but by my spirit."[1] When you settle back in that assurance and realize, "There is no need for me to battle any person or condition: It is not physical might or mental power that is needed—it is Thy Spirit, Father"; then, you no longer carry on a warfare against the flesh, that is, against the principalities and powers of this earth, because you have come into a conscious awareness

[1] Zechariah 4:6.

of the truth that only God is power. You are over-shadowed with the power of the Almighty and you have felt the descent of the Holy Ghost. Empowered from on High, the Spirit flows out from you, and through you, to all who come within range of your consciousness.

At the moment of the conception and birth of the Christ in you, you pass from being a human being to living in the Soul. The mind takes on its proper function as an instrument to be used, just as you use your body as a vehicle for your expression and activity. When you make that transition in consciousness, you do not lose your body. Even when you leave this plane, you will carry your body with you. However, it continually appears to improve in accord with your improved concept of body. You are never without a body, just as you are never without a mind, but now both the body and the mind become instruments of the Soul. The Soul imparts Itself to you through the mind, and then the body carries out Its orders and performs the functions of being. Every phase of your life is lived through the Spirit which emanates from the deep within you.

That is the meaning of the immaculate conception. It is the conception of the Christ in your conscious-ness and Its birth as a transformed life. The birth of the Christ will come into your individual experience when you make the transition from living through the mind to living through the Soul. Then you are no longer a human being: You are the Christ of God.

*   *   *

Says Deity Is Substance of All Form

A review of *God, the Substance of All Form*
Merab Eberle

From the *Journal Herald*, Dayton, Ohio,
October 3, 1959

This book, latest in the rapidly growing output of works by the contemporary mystic, Joel S. Goldsmith, holds that God is the substance of every form, the essence of what appears as mankind, plant, animal, mineral.

Mr. Goldsmith writes that God is universal consciousness, an absolute and all-inclusive perfection, the Infinite Cause embodying all form and effect.

Human consciousness, according to this author, is a fallen or erroneous state of consciousness which can be dissolved through recognition of God-consciousness as the truth of being. When it is dissolved, he says, the kingdom of God is revealed within the individual.

He writes: "The whole kingdom of God is within your own consciousness . . . and nothing—no group of people, no government, no kind of economy—can in any way enter your consciousness to prevent it from unfolding as your particular good."

This is the latest of several books by this author issued by the English publishers, L. N. Fowler and Company.

Harper and Brothers which has previously brought out his *The Art of Meditation* and *Practicing the Presence* will publish, November 1, Mr. Goldsmith's *The Art of Spiritual Healing*.

*   *   *

We shall be spending the holiday season at home in Hawaii and will remain there until the middle of January when we start on our 1960 schedule of travel.

Among the great blessings which have enriched consciousness this year are the new *God, the Substance of All Form, The Art of Spiritual Healing*, and *A Lesson to Sam*, and probably the great "pearl" without price for all Infinite Way students is to be found in the monthly *Letters* of June, August, September, October, and November, 1959. The serious study and practice of the principles embodied in these *Letters* will change the life and consciousness of any student.

This is the first holiday in the history of the world when man no longer need look forward to the establishment of peace on earth and good will to all men, for today this peace on earth and good will among men are already established on earth as they are in heaven, and what we shall witness in the coming years is but the unfolding of this spiritual state of peace, interpreting itself as real peace on earth, made manifest as good will among men.

Whatever discords remain among the nations of the world, whatever minor bits of warfare, or whatever of wrangling and disputes will only be the working out on the human plane of the peace that is already established in consciousness.

The world, however, will only become aware of this bit by bit and step by step, as this consciousness of harmony unfolds and discloses itself in human affairs. But those who are spiritually attuned will become aware of the fullness of the attained peace-consciousness in the degree that they realize that there is now another Consciousness at work in their being, in their bodies, in their business, and in their daily lives.

When you, individually, begin to perceive that *My* peace—the Christ-peace—has been given you, that *My* consciousness is operating in you, as you, through you, for you, and with you, permeating the experiences of all those who touch you on your daily pathway of life, you will, of course, be aware of this *My* peace which has now descended upon you and upon your affairs. Because of this you will begin to realize that this is becoming the experience of all mankind, even though those not spiritually attuned will not for awhile become aware of it. You will recognize it, however, because you understand that God is no respecter of persons and that, therefore, this Consciousness, which is now operating in your experience and going before you to make the crooked places straight, which is now appearing as your bread, meat, wine, and water, as your fortress and your high tower, is likewise the Consciousness which is now breaking through into universal experience and acceptance.

Do not be too hasty to publish these good tidings to those not prepared to receive them, but rather rejoice within yourself that in due time all the world will become as aware of the divine Presence as you now are. Any desire on your part to rush out and tell this to mankind is only catering to your ego, an evidence of a desire still remaining in you to be thought wise. That which you know in secret through your inner communion, God will shout from the housetops, so that you need not be a personal bearer of this message, and yet, as those come into your experience capable of receiving a spiritual impartation, a way will open up for you to bring to them this assurance and conviction.

Since we left Hawaii late in July, we have travelled from the west coast of the United States and Canada, across the continent to New York, and from there to England, Germany, Holland, and Switzerland; and everywhere there are signs of peace on earth and good will among men.

I cannot tell you of the two major signs that have been given, because I am not free to do this; but it has been made evident that *My* consciousness—the Christ-consciousness—is the consciousness of those who have attained the inner ear, and that *My* peace has been made evident in two major experiences and many contributory experiences, all bearing witness to the truth that the principle of Life is functioning on earth as it is in heaven.

Infinite Way students can contribute to the realization of this peace on earth by spending many quiet days during the holiday season in inner communion and thanksgiving that God's grace is functioning on earth. They can also contribute to the realization and acceptance of divine Grace by maintaining "in quietness and in confidence" that which has been revealed to them, to the end that this wondrous gift may be kept in sacred silence, so as to permit the voice of God to publish the news in human consciousness.